THE HIPPO CAMPUS

A step by step guide to get your business noticed, remembered and talked about with Stand Out Marketing.

ANDREW AND PETE

Copyright © 2016 Andrew and Pete

All rights reserved.

For everybody who gave us a shot.

About the Authors

Let's first deal with the Hippo in the room. Yes, there are 2 of us. We are Andrew and Pete, and we run the award winning marketing company called: *Andrew and Pete*. We come as one and we write as one. You can find out more about us at www.andrewandpete.com

*The Hippocampus - "The elongated ridges on the floor of each lateral ventricle of the brain, thought to be the centre of emotion, **memory**, and the autonomic nervous system."*

Contents

SECTION	PAGE
Welcome Note	6
Induction	9
SOM101: Understanding Marketing Today	29
SOM102: A Framework for Thinking Creatively	50
SOM103: Making Your Business Stand Out	82
SOM104: Inspiration	135
SOM105: Conclusion	159

Welcome Note

Hello, and welcome to The Hippo Campus.

We are so excited to have you reading this book, so if you are reading this now - which we guess you must be - we just wanted to say a big THANK YOU followed by a big WOOHOO. Hope you are as excited as we are?

This book has been in the making for a few years, (as it has taken time to consolidate all we have learned and practised in the field of Stand Out Marketing) into one easy to follow, easy to implement guide for you. But it is finally here!

Why is it called The Hippo Campus? We are going to get to that shortly, but for now we just wanted to quickly take you through how the book is supposed to be used.

The book follows a logical order separated into 4 main sections:

1. **Understanding Marketing Today.** This is a brief look into the history of marketing, so you understand where we have been, where

we are going, and why these principles are needed today.
2. **A Framework for Thinking Creatively.** This delves into your brand, and how you should be using your branding to think of ideas that make sense specifically to you.
3. **Thinking of Stand Out Ideas.** Once you have your brand nailed down, this section tells you how to use it, to come up with new and exciting ideas that will set you apart in your industry.
4. **Inspiration.** For the creative, and the non-creative, we all need to find inspiration. This section is going to tell you how, as well as how to keep that forward momentum to keep your business fresh.

Assignments. Just like a real university, each module comes with assignments to complete. This book was written to inspire action! Complete these assignments to actually put into practice what you learn. There is extremely little theory in the assignments, it is all working on your business to better it and make it remarkable.

Extra Resources and Graduation.
This is also more than a book. If you go to www.thehippocampusbook.com you'll find completely free resources, that have been put

together to complement this book, as well as up to date information, examples in practice and video content from us. Use all this, and once you have completed the book, download your Graduation Certificate.

So, are you ready to get going? We sure are! See you on the other side.

Andrew and Pete
Faculty Heads of Staff

Induction

Our moment of realisation that Stand Out Marketing works...

We got a phone call one bright, sunny Summer's day. OK, it's England - who are we kidding? It was probably raining!

Anyway, it went something like this...

The phone rings, "Hello, Andrew and Pete, how can I help...?" answers Pete.

"Hi, it's John Smith. I was wondering if we could meet up and discuss marketing my new venture....?"

[Note: this guy's real name isn't John Smith, if you hadn't worked that out already].

We aren't going to bore you with the full transcript, so let's skip ahead to the end of the conversation.

One thing you have to understand about us... Andrew is the Wikipedia of our business. Ask him anything about where we met a certain person, or where we are up to in a project with a client and he'll tell you. So after the conversation ended, Pete (who hasn't got a clue who John Smith is), turns to Andrew.

"Andrew, John Smith wants to meet to discuss marketing."
"Great... who's John Smith?" Andrew replies.
"He said we met him at a networking event."

Andrew, the Wikipedia of *Andrew and Pete*, was stumped. He didn't have a clue who John Smith was.

Here's why...

We had only spoken to John briefly for a couple of minutes over a year ago prior to this call and had no idea what he had been up to or even what he did. But he knew everything about us.

Little did we know, but John had been captivated by our 40 second speech at the networking event we were at and had been avidly following our newsletters and social media ever since, waiting for an opportunity to work together. Finally that opportunity came, and there he was on the phone a year later.

A year.

A full year that he had remembered us. A full year when no other marketing company he had met in between had come close to his vision of working with us. A full year and we hadn't even spent any time selling to him and yet here he was wanting our services. That's crazy!

This now happens all the time. People remember us because we do things a bit differently at Andrew and Pete.

It's moments like these that make us believe so much in the power of Standing Out. We Stood Out so much for John that a year later he still remembered us and wanted to work with us. It would have been sooner given the chance. All it took was being a bit different. No nurturing of leads, no sales meetings, just one act of Standing Out. Hard work forever pays. Or rather, Standing Out forever pays.

So...

The aim of this book is to teach you how to do the same thing; to fascinate your audience so much that they will remember you forever more, buy from you AND tell everyone else about you. What could sound better than that?!

> "STANDING OUT *FOREVER PAYS*."
>
> thehippocampusbook.com
> by @andrewandpete

Come on then Andrew and Pete, tell us why it is called 'The Hippo Campus'?

We thought you'd never ask.

The Hippocampus is the part of the brain responsible for memory, and as the 'marketing team' (that's you!) it's your job to lodge yourself right up in there in your target audience's brain!

But there's more to it than just being remembered. It's about creating an emotional pull. It's about being remembered for the right reasons, and it's about getting people to spread the word about you.

There's a perfect word that sums all this up.

When we are working with our clients we aim not to make them really good, not great, not even amazing!

Just simply, *remarkable*.

i.e. worth making a 'remark' about.

This use of the word remarkable comes from Seth Godin's book, 'The Purple Cow.' Great book, go read it and everything else by Seth - he's awesome! Or should we say, he's remarkable.

It's such a perfect word; it suggests being remembered for something positive, not just for being crazy or weird, but also that you are worth talking about.

'Stand Out' is all about differentiation, innovation, leadership, creativity, experiences, tribes, storytelling, and more than that - breaking the mould.

It's about being noticed, being remembered and being talked about.

Who has ever got to the top doing what everybody else is doing?

Nobody.

So how are you going to break the mould to reach the top? How are you going to Stand Out? This book is for anybody who wants to get away from the 'average'. It's for those who dare to be different and for those who dream to achieve something amazing.

Now, we're sure that's what everybody wants, right? Every business wants to get themselves noticed above their competition. But few we see are actually going out of their way to make that happen.

There's a few reasons why we think that happens.

The first is that the fear of people looking at us and judging us often outweighs the perceived benefits of doing something 'Stand Out'. That's fine, we are going to cover how you can Stand Out in a way that fits your business to a T.

The second is that those *perceived* benefits aren't *perceived* highly enough.

We have a diagram coming up a bit later in the book that is going to show you exactly how this all works, so believe us - when you can Stand Out and be remarkable in the right way (follow our process and you will) this is what is going to happen to you:

- You will get noticed ahead of all of your competition
    - You will get attention, and your audience will listen to what you have to say
    - You and your messages will be remembered (thus you will need fewer impressions to make a sale)
    - You will make immediate sales
    - You will get leads long after the impressions you made - much like John Smith
- You break through the world of indifference and attract your ideal audience who will become your loyal fans
    - You will repel those who are not your ideal audience so you don't waste time chasing them
- Your ideal clients will beg to work with you
- Your clients will spend more money with you and will be repeat customers
    - Your clients will also become your best sales force, all for free
- Collaborators will beg to work with you, employees for you
- Your reach will be catapulted ahead of your competition from all the free PR
- People will talk about how remarkable you are far and wide and you will get an ever-growing, exponential stream of leads knocking at your door

- Your position in the market will increase with a greater presence
  - Your credibility, likability, trust and respect will skyrocket
  - There will be a buzz around you and your company
- You will be able to uncouple people from using their favourite brands, and use you instead!

Imagine this for you and what it would mean to your business. No more chasing business, no more annoying clients and at last - you can sell at the prices you deserve.

This can all be yours: we have seen clients double their prices and double their clients in just three months using these techniques. Not to mention reducing their hours per week and having fun along the way.

Having fun is important too; marketing doesn't have to be chore! So many of our clients come to us thinking it is, and right now you might be thinking the same. We understand that. Most people go into business doing something they love or have skills in, and marketing is just an afterthought that seems like hard work. Well, we're here to change that too because Standing Out is all about becoming more of yourself.

"You don't have to change who you are, you have to become more of who you are." – *Sally Hogshead, branding expert.*

You're going to delve into what makes you and your company special, what your values are, and maximise those. The Hippo Campus isn't about being random and crazy. To Stand Out, it is about becoming more 'you'! This will be an enjoyable process...

What This Book Isn't

There is a ton of information and books written specifically to help you Stand Out, but they mainly focus on the business model as a whole. This is fine for start-ups but as a current business owner, already doing what you do, this is no good. You don't want to have to reinvent the wheel, start new businesses and basically... start again!

No, this book is for you if you're already on your path. You may have recently started, be a few months in or even ten/twenty years in business, it doesn't matter. This book is for you, and it's going to be ultra-practical. So get excited! We hate reading stuff that leaves you inspired, but doesn't tell you exactly how to do it, so this book is about looking at your existing company and processes and improving them to make your company Stand Out.

Standing Out is a marvellous thing, however, the problem is that it cannot be replicated by its very nature. Once done, it cannot be done again and have the same impact. If everyone does the same Stand Out activity, then it will no longer 'Stand Out'.

With this in mind, this book is not going to tell you what to do, but rather, the exact process we use with our clients to make your business Stand Out in its own right. It's about being original, looking at your own values and skills and above all - getting creative.

"But I'm not a creative person, 'Andrew and Pete'. I don't have any ideas".

We've heard that one before, believe us. Don't worry, we've got you covered. If your favourite colour is grey, and your favourite ice cream flavour is vanilla... this book's aim is to get even you thinking creatively about your business too.

[Side note: *Andrew's favourite ice cream flavour is vanilla, and he thinks labelling it boring is unfair, but hey-ho*]

It's the same for everyone, you need to Stand Out to win.

> Take a photo of this and Tweet using #hippocampusbook

> "IT'S THE SAME FOR EVERYONE, YOU NEED TO *STAND OUT TO WIN*."
>
> thehippocampusbook.com
> by @andrewandpete

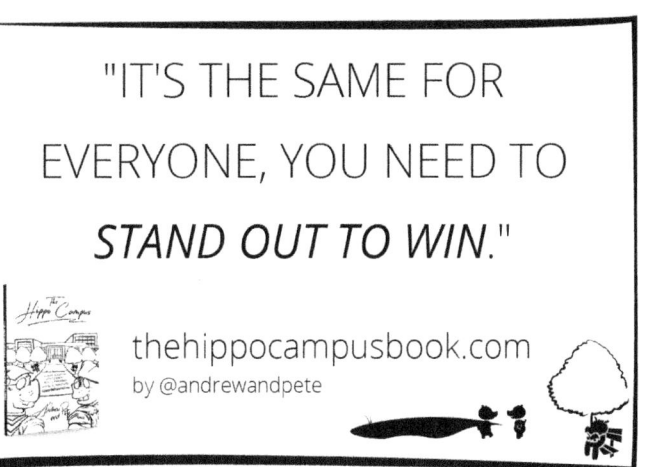

How This Book is Supposed to be Used

With that in mind we want this book to be a challenge to you. Not a challenge to read - we'll try to keep it fun! But rather we challenge you to take up the principles of this book and Stand Out. There are so many boring adverts and businesses these days that they all just merge into one and get ignored…

That is until one day you come across something super exciting, something that makes you stop and stare, point it out to everyone you know, take photos, share… and buy. Something so awesome that you will never forget it. That's the power of Stand Out

Marketing. That's what we are going to help you achieve and we believe every business, including yours, has huge potential if you are willing to go the extra mile.

We are going to give you a step by step process on how to Stand Out against all of your competition and grow your business like never before.

The book comes with assignments and also offers you further reading and useful tools to help you. This is called the Graduation Pack, which you can access at www.thehippocampusbook.com. It is also constantly updated so this book isn't just a book, but a lifelong learning companion. Once you have 'graduated' this class then you also get to join the elite group of other successful entrepreneurs who have also passed!

Why Small Businesses Actually Have an Advantage Here

We believe that small businesses have the biggest potential, which is why our tagline for our membership site *atomic* is "Marketing for the Small but Mighty". As a small business, you don't have to answer to anyone else. You don't have report to a board of directors or seek approval for an idea. You can be as creative as you want and as ballsy as you like.

In this day and age where you can work from anywhere with just a laptop, there are no limits to your success and every advantage to be had over larger companies stifling in death by consensus.

Big businesses are stale. As fancy as they can get with their big marketing budgets, they still need a mass market to support them, and for that they need to conform to the average. This can often limit and stifle innovation.

The small business is agile, quick to react, quick to take on feedback and improve and be more personable. It can scale up and down in size with cloud technology and take on new clients and communicate anywhere in the world. But most importantly, it has the ability to get creative and Stand Out. There are no limits, apart from the ones you place on yourself - all of which we aim to break through in this book.

What we are basically saying is that as small businesses, to grow and to scale, we each must be willing to be a bit of a rule breaker and stick our necks out to get *ahead* (pun very much intended).

Yes, it takes a little bit more effort at first, but follow this process and you'll end up putting in far less effort than you would running a struggling average business.

Small businesses often don't know how to get themselves out there and Stand Out. They often have a skill or a passion, but they don't know how to market that. So to be on the safe side they either look back in time, or look to see what everyone else in their market is doing, which results in either old-fashioned, out-dated marketing ideas or simply copying the competition, neither of which are effective.

As a new business, you have to consider many things at once, and it's easy to let marketing slip to the bottom of your to do list. You need to open your mind to the idea that marketing is more than just doing some flyers.

Comfort Blanket Marketing

First we must break free of what we call comfort blanket marketing.

A lot of entrepreneurs start a business and they think that their marketing is done once they have a nice flyer, a pretty website, a brochure to hand out and a branded item (usually in the form of pens, stress balls and keyrings - like people's keys are really missing your logo on a white background)!

And to a degree, yes, this will help. But all too often, people use these things as a comfort blanket. If they have them - their marketing is done. If they don't - they hide away because they don't have these things.

However... these things aren't marketing. At least not on their own. So stop thinking of marketing as 'stuff' you either get designed or printed, and start thinking of marketing as creative ways to get and hold the attention of your audience.

So Who Are Andrew and Pete?

We're about to get to the good stuff, but before we do, we just wanted to introduce ourselves and tell you a bit more of our story. Yes, you are a couple of pages in now, but better late than never as they say.

It's a quick story, promise...

We aren't quite as famous as Bono, Madonna or Rihanna... yet. We do have last names.

We're Andrew Pickering and Peter Gartland and our company believe it or not, is called: Andrew and Pete.

The bromance started when we randomly got placed in the same halls at university and bonded over our shared passion for one day ~~ruling the world~~ running a successful business empire.

When we left university we then had a decision to make: do we find a comfortable graduate job or do we try to make it on our own in the big bad world?

We decided to go for it of course, BUT we had a problem...

We were young, inexperienced, and Andrew wanted to move to the other side of the country (Newcastle upon Tyne) to live with his girlfriend, Vicky.

This meant we had to start up our marketing company in a city we barely knew, with no money, and no business contacts whatsoever.

We invested in a website, but the developer gave up halfway through. Ouch. So we dug deep and invested the rest of what little savings we had in another more expensive web development company...

What could possibly go wrong?

Unbelievably they also ripped us off and didn't give us our money back! We felt the weight of the world come crashing down on us.

By this point we had wasted months of our time, we had no website, no confidence in web developers, no client base, and we had spent all of our savings.

Even worse - it was at the time of the worst financial crisis in decades... and finally to top it off, Business Link (who funded many websites and marketing investments in the area) had been shut down, so there was no funding for marketing services, and no one in the area wanted to spend any money, especially on marketing.

Great.

So what did we do? How could we compete with all these bigger marketing companies, with all their fancy marketing materials? How could we come back from this crushing waste of time and money?

We could have given up, got a job, taken the easy route. Sounds like a perfectly sensible thing to do right?

But we didn't, we dug deep and got creative.

With nothing to live on we needed to act, and fast... if you've paid attention up to this point of the book, you can probably guess we are going to say we invested in Stand Out Marketing.

BINGO.

We learned quickly that if we were going to be successful we had to do stuff that was going to make us Stand Out from all the established, experienced companies. More importantly with little budget...

OK no budget.

We needed our own marketing to be efficient and effective. So we named our business 'Andrew and Pete', started doing things differently, and started teaching our clients how to do STAND OUT marketing to get themselves noticed too.

We got out there as much as possible and did things like taking indoor fireworks and party poppers to networking events. We did everything we could to get noticed, and it worked.

People started to notice us, wanted to be a part of what we had to offer, and also started referring work to us - great! :)

We knew what we were doing was working, but as we got to Year 2 and Year 3 of our business we had people like John Smith (remember him from earlier on in the book?) contacting us a full year after meeting us to hire us!

Fast forward to now (early 2016), and we have worked with hundreds of businesses, we work from a really nice office, collaborate with world leading experts, have won awards and we are paid to talk in public about our marketing expertise.

We 100% believe though that all this stemmed from those first few months in business, up against the 'big boys' and being forced to differentiate in order to get noticed, be remembered and get talked about.

This doesn't happen without huge sacrifice but we believe that:

"Entrepreneurship is living a few years of your life like most people won't, so that you can spend the rest of your life like most people can't." Anonymous.

We are on an ambitious journey, coming very far, very fast. We think it is down to our ambition and hard work ethic... but more importantly, letting our creative juices flow and Standing Out.

So buckle up, we are getting going now. Your first module is about to begin.

SOM101:
Understanding Marketing Today

Marketing Has Changed

First we are going to take you down memory lane.

We are going to ask you to think differently about marketing a business today, and forget a lot of what you already know, but firstly you need to understand why what used to work, doesn't work anymore.

Why? Because the world has changed in such a way that old school methods of advertising and marketing either don't work, or are now less effective. Importantly though, because these types of marketing have been done for so long, and in the past worked so well, it is often these types of marketing that people turn to when setting up their business.

Most people set up their business because they have a passion or skill; what they are not, is marketers. So they tend to do what they know and get some flyers and a website and business cards and think that the marketing is done. Don't be one of those people!

An understanding then is important, not only of what worked in the past, but more importantly why it worked, and why it won't work anymore.

The history of marketing is much longer and much more complicated than this short summary, but the aim of this is to give you a general understanding of how the world has changed with marketing, and how marketing has changed the world.

Interruption Marketing

As society developed, production economies and products were being mass produced left, right and centre, so the key marketing strategy at this time was to produce products cheaply and in bulk, and to get as many people to know about a product as possible. The best way to do this? By interrupting people.

Print, radio and TV all revolutionised marketing, in that order. First there was print: with advances in the printing press companies could print adverts, flyers and posters en mass and distribute them to lots of people. Then came the radio and radio advertising, which made reaching even more people even easier. Then finally TV advertising took this to a whole other level. TV provided a rich, sensory, captivating experience whereby the whole nation would sit round the TV as a family and watch whatever was on. The lack of channels meant that the audiences were huge. Companies would spend millions on TV advertising, and it was worth it; the profits on cheaply made products were large, because TV advertising could give them the necessary exposure to the masses. It was mass produced goods being sold to the masses - average products for average people. But why did this work?

Put simply, in those days we didn't have Google.

Nowadays if we have a problem or we want to buy something we can just search online for it or come across a solution on one of the many social networks, but back then advertisements were the only way of really knowing what was out there. So in this sense, the ads were actually useful to people - worth watching to know what was out there to be able to 'keep up with the Joneses'.

This meant that the big players won – the more distribution you could buy, the more you could sell and then the more distribution you could buy again in a merry cycle of prosperity.

The key thing all these had and still have in common though is that they rely on interrupting people.

Nobody really reads a magazine, listens to the radio, or watches TV just for the ads.

Small Business Interruption Marketing

Although small businesses could never afford the big TV advertising costs, they too were using interruptive methods such as flyer drops, cold-calls and local advertising, and this used to work well. Sometimes advertising was actually welcomed, as it was a good way to find out about new local shops, products and services.

The Meltdown

Picture this - you are alone in an empty room. One person walks up to you and starts talking to you. Do you listen? Yes, probably. Now somebody else comes up to you and starts talking to you at the same time. It becomes a little harder to concentrate on what the first person is saying. And now a third has joined in, and a fourth, and a fifth. Eventually you have hundreds of people trying to talk to you, but you can't hear them anymore. Not only can you not hear them, but it is annoying, and you try to drown them out and ignore them. This is exactly what happened with marketing. With so many companies advertising and 'selling', people got fed up, and drowned them out. We almost don't even think about it anymore.

Marketing materials are part of our everyday life; we receive them through the post, on our way to work, at work, at home, and even in our leisure time. We don't really mind receiving them, but we are indifferent to them. Which poses a problem for marketers. No attention.

Next time you go to work in the morning, count how many adverts, logos and sales messages you see on your way, all dying for your attention. The sad truth for marketers is that most will be forgotten, because we are just too used to seeing them.

The Launch of the Internet

The launch of the Internet was the first major shift in marketing for centuries. Some people will argue TV should count as a major shift, but TV, like its predecessors, relied on interrupting people. The Internet provided something completely different that the marketing world had never seen before.

When it first launched, it did add to the interruption initially, with annoying pop-ups, and banner ads here, there and everywhere. Nobody knew how to use it at first, and so just used it as another sales medium. But what was unique was that the Internet provided consumers with a wealth of information.

This shift now meant that we didn't need the ads to find out what was out there, we could find it ourselves on demand. Adverts were no longer of use, but rather an annoyance. With a click of a few buttons, consumers can find the answers they are looking for, and the products they need.

Marketers needed to make sure their products and their services were the ones that were found when searching online, and Search Engine Optimisation was born. Niching and targeting also became all the more important. People were searching for specific things for their needs; they didn't want generic products for everyone. If you could niche and target your offering, then when people were searching for something specific, you had the best chance of being found and bought. Specific answers to specific individual problems flipped traditional 'average products for average people' methods on its head. So the Internet changed the marketing landscape forever, but the biggest change was still to come...

Web 2.0 - The customers talk back

During the Internet's infancy, web pages were static informational pages, but as the technology progressed, websites became interactive, and it gave users a voice, in the form of 'user generated content.' The rise of comments, reviews, blogging and social media gave customers a power that they had never possessed - the power to talk back. Prior to this point, marketing was a one-way direction. Businesses spoke to the customers; customers chose to listen or ignore.

Now, marketing is a conversation - people will talk about you publicly whether you want them to or not. People can comment on how good or bad you are, whenever they want, and it is visible to the world. Marketers have lost control and the old techniques don't work anymore.

Now, when you're looking for information, you ask friends and people you trust, and search online to find out more. Traditional interruptive "salesy" marketing no longer works – it's lost its value. The information online gives a broader view of what's out there, the customer is in control and the options available to them have never been greater. You don't have to wait for an advert to show you what you need - you can find it yourself whenever you want.

For the companies, this means that their adverts are no longer useful – people actively avoid them, ignore them, scroll past, fast-forward or close down. Studies have even been done that found our eyes have been trained not to look at the right hand side of a screen anymore, because that's where online adverts traditionally appear on websites.

Side point: How many of your 'Calls to Action' are on the right side of your website?

This creates a massive paradigm shift and you can't just keep hammering your message home using TV and print adverts the way you might have done in the past. This principle applies if you're at a networking event, giving out flyers or have an advert in a local magazine.

Simply presenting your product, highlighting the features and benefits and asking people to buy will not work, unless it's a revolutionary item or the person you target is ready to buy at that exact moment, which is usually 1% of your audience. The other 99% will just be annoyed.

Marketers tend to respond by getting louder, resulting in consumers being bombarded to the point where they barely even notice something amongst all the white noise.

We took a ten minute car journey counting all the advertising messages we could see including billboards, shop front ads, and posters etc. Guess how many we counted? 50? 150? No, 300! Wow. That's not even counting all the car brands that we drove past.

Spend a few minutes online and you will find the same: promoted search results, sidebar ads, pop-ups, suggested websites, ads in social media feeds, ads in your email inbox and on your phone... you just can't escape ads.

Web 2.0 opened up all kinds of opportunities for businesses, and many issues too, but the main point is that marketing is now a conversation online, and you can use these online websites to interact and engage with your audience in a way that isn't interruptive, but in a way that is valued.

Content Marketing and Permission Marketing

Post Web 2.0, content marketing and permission marketing are two forms of marketing that have come to the forefront. Businesses using content marketing rely on the fact that people are now actively searching for information, so ensure their business is found by publishing relevant and useful content (note: NOT sales messages). By being useful, and showing your expertise in an area, you can build trust and build a relationship. Customers will come to you for your products and services, rather than you having to go out and find them. You'll often see this being referred to as 'inbound marketing'.

Marketing guru/expert/blogger/god Seth Godin coined the phrase 'Permission Marketing'. This is where you can get people to grant you permission to keep in touch with them by opting in to your free subscription. You tease them in, by offering actual value (note: again NOT sales messages), and keep in touch with them, nurturing the relationship, and providing constant value in your communications. Once again you build yourself as the expert in their eyes, so when they are ready to buy your product/service, they will at least consider you.

The Future

Though traditional methods of marketing can still be successful if done right, consumers have now changed forever. Nobody can really predict what is next for the marketing world, but we can analyse trends to see what's working and what isn't.

We are on a massive cusp of technological and communication advances and those who stand still are going to be left behind.

It's now easier than ever to get online and voice your opinion and ideas, but it is also harder than ever to get attention and be noticed above all the noise.

It's easier than ever to share things you like online, and if worthy, easier than ever to go viral. It's easier than ever to find whatever you want. It's easier than ever to switch providers. It's easier than ever to review thousands of these providers, products and services before you buy.

These conditions lead to companies getting the attention they deserve, good or bad. If you are remarkable, then we live in a world where it is easier than ever for people to make a remark about you, to share your message.

On the flip side however, it's also harder than ever not to be drowned out in all the noise.

The fact is, you can no longer afford to be average. You are competing against the world.

> Take a photo of this and Tweet using #hippocampusbook

> # "YOU CAN NO LONGER AFFORD TO BE *AVERAGE*."
>
> thehippocampusbook.com
> by @andrewandpete

Business is now an Olympic sport! If you are not the best in your field then you won't win; you will get left behind and you will struggle. There are seven billion people on this planet and, with access to the Internet and cheap travel and low distribution costs, competition has got a lot harder. Why buy your services when there is someone better, cheaper, faster than you somewhere else on the planet?

The point is this: there is a need for Stand Out Marketing now more than ever.

What is Stand Out Marketing?

It's a concept that's relevant to different businesses in different ways. Stand Out Marketing is **not** a one size fits all approach. Each company has its own unique brand values and an "upper crazy limit" on how far it'll go. Stand Out Marketing isn't about being daft or crazy just for the sake of it though, rather it is about finding that inner remarkability that only you have, and having the courage to show off your uniqueness to the world. It's about showing you and your company's unique authentic self, getting creative, and above all... having fun. We don't want to make marketing a chore for you.

In a nutshell it is all about being noticed, being remembered and being talked about.

So this book is going to give you a step by step process to help you realise what your authentic self is, and how to use that to make your company and your marketing Stand Out.

The Discus Model: Get Discussed

The Hippo Campus book is based on this principle...

"By doing something in a STAND OUT way, we allow our businesses the opportunity to get noticed, get remembered, and get talked about."

An easy way to remember this is with the Discus Model, where the harder you throw (i.e. the more you can apply these Stand Out principles), the more you are discussed (get it?).

THE DISCUS MODEL

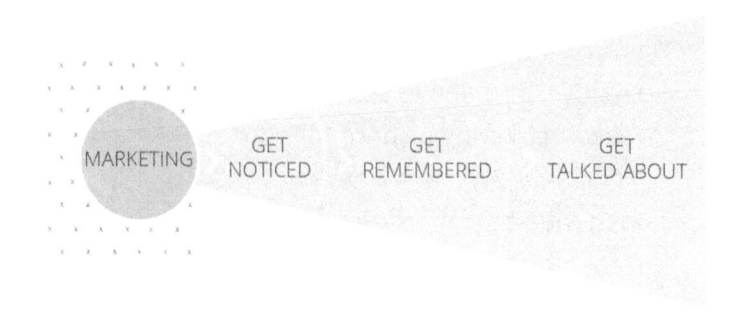

MARKETING → GET NOTICED → GET REMEMBERED → GET TALKED ABOUT

There are three areas you can land your business in... NOTICED, REMEMBERED AND TALKED ABOUT.

It's not an overly complex diagram, but we should be thinking about marketing with these three things in mind, and applying them to everything we do.

It's a scale from good to better to great. Getting noticed is good, being remembered is even better, but in this digital age, things start happening when we get talked about for the right reasons.

Let us give you an example.

Scenario 1

You have an office in a city centre and are walking down the street towards it. It is crowded with people, lined with shops, littered with adverts, billboards, people holding signs and charity collectors trying to get you to sign up for a regular donation. All trying to interrupt your day to get you to do what they want you to do.

In amongst all the chaos you see Iron Man selling hot dogs.

Stick with us...

Iron Man selling hot dogs gets your attention. You are out for lunch anyway. 'I bought a hot dog from Iron Man' is a cool story to tell. Sold. Iron Man got noticed, he got your business.

But what if you weren't out for lunch? What if you noticed him, but had no reason to buy? Would you remember him next time you did need lunch? Maybe, but it's a gamble.

Scenario 2

How about this, you are again walking down your street on the way to work 8am in the morning. You've had breakfast already.

It's a bit early for hot dogs, but instead Iron Man is giving out 'Super Power Coffee' for free. He has just launched 'Super Dogs' and wants to drum up some loyalty. On the cup it says 'Don't throw me out, come back after 12pm with the empty cup for another free refill and a half price double dog.'

You say thank you, go to work, drink the coffee, and instead of throwing it out, you leave the empty cup on your desk. A constant reminder.

This time come 12pm, Iron Man remains fresh in your mind. You've remembered him. You are hungry and decide to go check out how good Iron Man's hot dogs really are. He got your attention, and you remembered him. Great.

But are you talking about him yet?

Again maybe, but it's a gamble. You had a busy day; you've not had time to stop, and have only talked to three people since 8am.

Scenario 3

You are going to work again. It's 8am again. Iron Man has the same offer on as he did on scenario 2, but this time he isn't alone.

Nope, the whole of The Avengers is standing next to him. Captain America, Hulk, Thor, Black Widow and even Hawkeye.

Yes, even Hawkeye!

They are doing free photo opportunities, and handing out vouchers that say 'If our hot dogs are good enough for The Avengers, why not try them with YOUR TEAM. Feed 10 for the price of 5, for a super-hero lunch.'

What do you do now? You go get your photo taken with The Avengers, and now you have the perfect answer to the question that gets asked every morning.

'Morning, how are you?'
'I'm great, I just got my photo taken with The Avengers, they have this lunch offer on if anyone fancies it'.

You also have social media fodder here. You can picture it right?

Just met The Avengers this morning. Upload photo. Post.

In this scenario, Iron Man Selling hot dogs hasn't just got noticed, hasn't just been remembered but is actually being talked about in the real world and online.

The Benefits of Stand Out Marketing.

There's this thing with businesses that is hard to explain, but you'll know what we mean. Some businesses just have a *buzz*.

Some businesses, you can just see things happening for them. And that is because they are successfully being noticed, being remembered and being talked about.

Word of Mouth is stronger than ever. We know businesses who swear they don't need marketing, because…

'All our sales come from word of mouth'.

Newsflash: Word of mouth IS marketing. Most of these businesses have an awesome product/service with loyal fans, but imagine if they invested in getting even MORE word of mouth. Especially in this digital age we are living in, getting talked about is easier than ever, and more effective than ever.

Word of mouth is getting talked about, it is that indescribable buzz. And once you have it, doors swing open off their hinges.

ASSIGNMENT

Task 1: We want you to start being aware of the hectic clutter that we live in today. So your assignment is to basically count the number of adverts and logos and promotions that you see on your next journey out.

Notice the billboards, the shop windows, the posters, bus stop adverts, adverts on the side of buses, the company vans, the branded up lorries, the people on the high street trying to get your attention... the ads on your phone when you are trying to find some directions or place names, the Wi-Fi login page adverts, the push notifications as you go past a shop... and so on.

In fact, why not Tweet us what you find? You will be shocked at just how many there are. Our username is @andrewandpete and the hashtag is #hippocampusbook.

Now, understand that this is what you are up against. All this noise that you have to compete with.

Task 2: A day later, write down as many as you can remember. Unless you have a photographic memory, you'll find not many of them got stuck in your hippocampus. Ask yourself, from the ones you do remember, why did they stick?

This is just a warm up exercise to get you thinking. Assignments from here on in, we are going to be directly working on your business.

SOM102:
A Framework for Thinking Creatively

Not all Stand Out Marketing ideas are right for everybody

When you start to work on your marketing with The Hippo Campus in mind, it's important to make good decisions, as what you do needs to resonate with who you want to actually buy from you.

You don't want to get your bits out and do a naked photoshoot for no good reason! Especially in winter.

This section is all about setting the foundations of a solid brand to help come up with Stand Out Marketing ideas that actually align with your brand and your customers, rather than just being weird or crazy (or getting naked) for no reason.

Stand Out Marketing ideas don't just appear out of thin air and work.

Not the good ones anyway.

They appear through having a super-strong connection to what your brand is all about. This works whether you are amazingly creative, or not at all.

If you are amazingly creative it will give your ideas a framework to constrain and develop where necessary, and if you are not creative at all, it will point you in the right direction of what you should be thinking about.

Because, like we said earlier, when you're not sure where to start, it's all too easy to just go with the flow of what everyone else is doing, rather than taking the time to think hard and get creative.

"There seems to be no limit to which some people will go to avoid the effort and labour that is associated with [thinking]." *Thomas Edison*

We're going to outline the best ways to come up with great ideas that suit your business and industry, but you have to be committed and prepared to do some thinking!

If you don't your marketing will never be any different to everybody else, and you won't Stand Out.

So how do we go about creating this framework then…?

It Starts with the Brand

Your brand isn't just your logo, your slogan, your website or your marketing materials. We like to think of it as this: "Your brand is the gut feeling people get when working with your company." You can't control it or force it on people, they decide it themselves by what they say about you when you're not in the room. The good news is, you can influence it, which we'll get to.

But for now, think of your brand as the gut feeling people get when working with you, as well as what they say about you behind your back.

For many small businesses and sole traders your brand is the same as your own personal brand, because people talk about you the same way they talk about your business, and often your brand values are aligned (more on brand values later too).

That's why we say Stand Out Marketing can be pure, because it can be a way of maximising and showing off your personality. Sure not everyone will like it (you're not friends with everybody), but those that do will find that your personalities will align, creating a much stronger bond of trust and increasing the likelihood of you working together. For sole traders, the personality of the business is usually your personality, for teams and bigger businesses you need to give the business its own brand, and ensure everyone on the team knows what it stands for. Either way, when you know wholeheartedly what your brand is, then every decision you make from there on in will be much easier and true to yourself and your company.

We're going to talk about developing your own brand through your brand values in just a minute because it is the crucial cornerstone many forget, but before you do that, it is vital that you understand this…

Average Leads to Indifference

When making Stand Out decisions, you do need to be confident.

Often people are afraid of offending others, being laughed at or even put on a pedestal.

How often have you been to a networking event where the attendees are hesitant to get up and do their 60 second pitch? Isn't that the whole point of networking?! If you want people to buy from you they first have to know you exist! So don't be afraid.

The first thing you need to do is avoid death by consensus. Stop asking everybody around you for their views on your business. Choose a few people whose opinion you trust and go to them, ensuring they understand your brand first, but stop asking everybody and their mothers. This will only lead to an average response, which leads to an average result, and that's the last thing you want. Nobody can fall in love with an average brand. Take the world's most profitable brand, Apple - they have immensely loyal brand advocates... and they have people who can't stand them. It comes down to this:

Average leads to indifference!

> Take a photo of this and Tweet using #hippocampusbook

> **"AVERAGE LEADS TO**
> *INDIFFERENCE."*
>
> thehippocampusbook.com
> by @andrewandpete

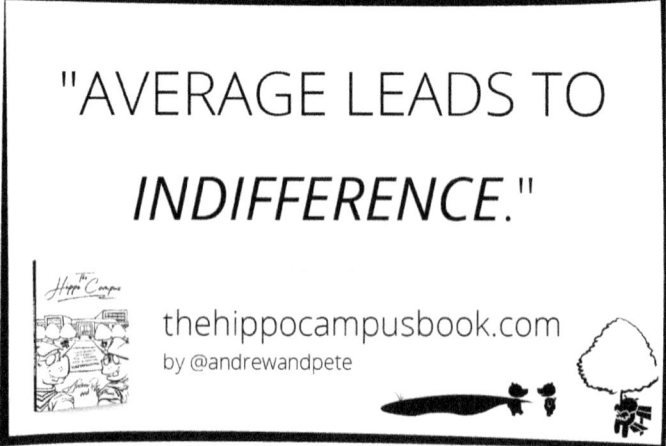

You may find that the people you're asking don't know the full story and will just tell you what they think you want to hear. 'Yes Men' aren't helpful. And there's always a danger of them trying to help by coming up with random new ideas that don't align to your goals or brand or audience. Everyone has different perspectives and think they're experts.

Asking advice from everyone you know is counterproductive, because it slows you down and can lead to self-doubt and analysis paralysis.

Successful entrepreneurs know who they are and what they do, and are comfortable with that. The key is not to spend too much time overanalysing. Know your target market, know your brand values, and push the safe boundaries to the limit.

Most business owners out there don't Stand Out because they're afraid to. This is fantastic because it means you can!

If everyone else is being average, this means that actually there's more competition for being average. They're all trying to do the same thing and competing with each other. So think of it this way:

Being safe is the new risky.

An industry we see which falls into this trap a lot is surprisingly, marketing agencies. If you think about it, on the face of it, most of them are the same. Amazingly sleek, beautiful websites, professional design, great abstract photos, maybe a page on their team, they've won an award, and here's the clincher... they will probably have an alternative name like 'Blue Lemon' or 'Hairy Pepper' or something random to make them sound 'creative.' That all sounds great right?

BUT EVERYBODY IS DOING THAT. It is what we have come to expect from that industry, so it doesn't catch us by surprise, and it doesn't really say anything about them that will differentiate them from the competition.

It is much better to develop a brand based on YOUR unique values, rather than based on what is expected.

If you base a brand on what is expected, you just become another business in your industry. It is going to be really tough to get that traction, you will blend into the background and you won't Stand Out.

Don't follow the crowd - it's got more competition!

Do something different and it will pay off.

A lady who did just that is Andrea Vahl, a Facebook marketing expert and author. She could have set up her agency like everybody else, and blended into the background, but instead she built her brand from what was unique to her.

See Andrea has a secret weapon, her other passion in improv comedy. So instead of teaching people Facebook marketing strategies as herself (which is what everybody else is doing), she started teaching Facebook marketing strategies as Grandma Mary, a slightly cranky Grandma who loves Facebook, spreading the message that "If Grandma Mary can do it, you can too."

She goes all out as well... wig, costume, voice and even walk! It's hilarious, but the content is just as informative, it is just delivered in a way that is memorable and entertaining.

Andrea's success as Grandma Mary is incredible, she is known as a leading expert on Facebook worldwide, talks at conferences all over the world, and was named as one of the 50 favourite online influencers by Entrepreneur.com

Developing Your Brand Values

To start thinking about your branding, the most logical place to start is with your brand values.

Remember, your brand is what other people think of you: you can't tell people what it is, but you can influence it.

To influence it you must first know what you want other people to think of you!

So you need to answer this question:

"What 3-5 words or phrases would you like somebody to use to describe your business?"

Baseline Brand Values

When we start doing this exercise with clients, they initially come up with what we call 'Baseline Brand Values.' These are values such as:
- Professional
- Friendly
- Helpful
- Knowledgeable
- Good customer service

They all sound good, right? But the big problem with these Baseline Values is that EVERYBODY USES THEM. How many businesses have you come across that say they offer a 'professional, friendly service' and pride themselves on 'good customer service?' Who wouldn't want to say that? So if you base your whole brand on Baseline Values, again all you get is an average brand that just adds to the noise in an already noisy world.

Baseline brand values do have a place but they're only the scratching the surface.

You may find Baseline Values are industry specific too. For example, a marketing company being 'creative' is pretty standard across the board, and therefore should be a baseline value if you are in that industry. A graphic designer saying they are creative should be a given right? But being 'creative' isn't the norm across all industries, it might not be a baseline value for say a lawyer, or gardener, or electrician for example.

So write down your baseline brand values, but look deep for Stand Out Brand Values too.

Stand Out Brand Values

Stand Out Brand Values are values that aren't standard across the board. They are values that are unique to your business and industry. Remember, it doesn't just have to be adjectives, it can be what you stand for, or how you want to come across.

Stand Out Brand Values could include:
- Funny
- Empowering women
- Ambitious
- Artistic
- Organised
- For FTSE 100 companies only
- For employees in the tech sector
- Passionate
- Understanding
- Sexy
- Inspirational
- Young and trendy
- Old fashioned
- Controversial
- Social
- Risky
- The list goes on...

Can you see how these are different to Baseline Values?

Brands based on Baseline Values will just blend into the background, as what they are trying to say about themselves is no different to the majority of their competition. Whereas brands based on Stand Out values, do just that... Stand Out, and in the upcoming modules, when you start making marketing and business decisions based on these Stand Out values, you'll be making decisions that cause your business to Stand Out too.

Deciding on Your Brand Values.

Deciding on your brand values isn't a two minute job. You need to take some real time out to develop and think about how you want to be perceived, and narrow it down to three to five Stand Out Brand Values to live by...

This is what we do...

Get a blank sheet of paper (note: not a blank Word document, or spreadsheet, an actual piece of paper) and write down all the words you would like somebody else to describe your business as.

Go for maybe 25-50 minutes as a minimum to get started.

Now, go through the list and mark off any that would be classed as Baseline Values, and put them to one side.

Now what we usually do is create groups of values that mean similar things. For example 'artistic', and 'creative' you may think are similar so can be grouped together. Likewise: 'empowering women' and 'inspirational', or 'funny' and 'trendy'. From these groups select a value that you think best sums up the group as a whole, and voila... your brand values emerge. For each category, choose the word that best sums it up, this is your 'Headline Stand Out Value'.

The easiest way to do this is to write down each word again in a list. If the word is similar to another put them next to each other. If completely different write it on another line, leaving some space in between.

So one category of similar words for us, for example, was that we wrote down things like: for small businesses and entrepreneurs, accessible, practical, affordable, help as many as possible, friendly, curators, overly helpful. The overarching Headline Stand Out Value becomes 'accessible'. This is one of our brand values, because we have a passion to help those that don't have big marketing budgets or access to world leading advice. We want to help as many people as possible as much as we can and so one way to do that is to make ourselves accessible in everything we do. Where time permits, we give people as much of our time and expertise as possible. This brand value gave us the idea for '*atomic*' - our marketing support membership site, and also the idea of weekly webinars so that our members can have as much access to us as possible.

When your brand values are clear, you start to make smarter decisions.

We say aim for three (max five) brand values because anymore and you risk diluting the brand. You can't be all things to all people. Besides, three is easier to remember!

Summary of Brand Values:
This is how you want to be perceived

At this point now, you should know what your brand values are (i.e. how you want to be perceived).

These three to five words or phrases are now going to form key marketing decisions going forward. So it is important that you think this through, and stick with them. Every decision you make has to be aligned with your brand and your brand values. If you don't, then your message is diluted and word of mouth will not spread about you.

The only thing left to add to our framework now is to look at who we want to work with.

Your Avatar - who do you want to help, and want to love you

The next thing you need to do is work out exactly who it is you want to help.

Remember you can't be all things to all people. And the more you can niche down the better.

One of the most asked questions we get about marketing is "How far should I target/niche down?" and "I work with X, Y and Z, will focus on X but not alienate Y and Z."

We get it, and to be 100% honest, it is something we struggled with too. Picking a target audience is hard, and shouldn't be taken lightly.

So here's an analogy we use to think about target audiences, to help you niche down too.

Because even though it can be hard, having that perfect customer in mind is so important when thinking about Stand Out Marketing, because not only does your marketing have to be in line with your brand values, it has to resonate with somebody.

When you know exactly who you are trying to be noticed by, remembered by, and talked about to:
- Your marketing becomes easier
- You make better decisions
- You can Stand Out to those people by simply being 'for them'
- You can compete better online
- You can improve your offering for them (and hence raise prices)
- You are more likely to be found online
- You are more likely to get referrals to perfect customers
- ...the list goes on.

Introducing: The Dartboard Analogy for Target Audiences

Think of your whole audience as a dartboard. In the middle sits your perfect customer, your avatar. You should know your avatar's name, job, income, where they hang out, what they do for fun, what their problems are etc. This should be the person you enjoy working with most or who your product is for, and who you can help the most. Decide on and flesh out your avatar.

The problem with this is that people think there are not enough people in the world like their avatar to buy from them. However, you are only seeing once piece of the dartboard.

Just because somebody isn't 100% like your avatar, doesn't mean they won't find what you are selling applicable to them. In fact, all the other bits of the dartboard are potential customers too.

Let's look at an example...

This is a bit simplified and we would recommend you flesh out your avatar a bit more than this, but a local hair salon may decide their avatar is: 'A glamorous female in her 40s, who cares about her appearance and has a good job, so therefore spends a bit extra on her hair.'

Their marketing is therefore focussed around solely attracting these kinds of people. However, who else probably still buys from this salon?

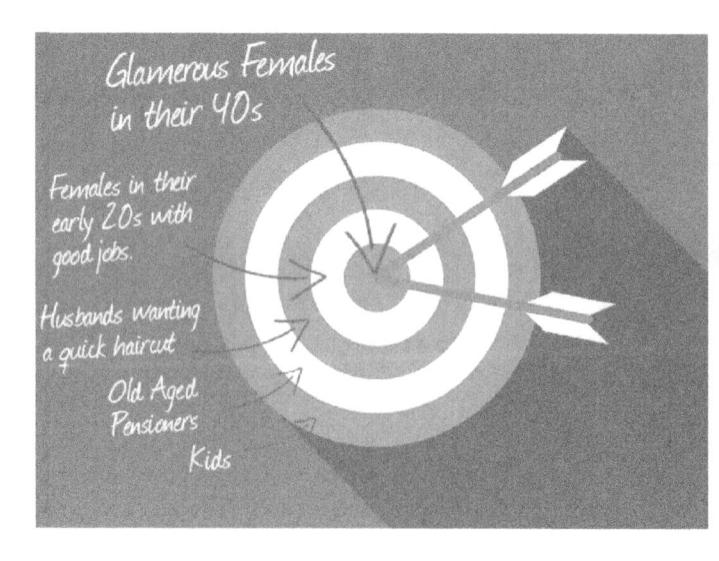

All these segments could buy from the salon anyway, as the salon's marketing may still attract them too.

For example... females in their early 20s with good jobs may be attracted by the high end imagery the salon uses, and wouldn't mind spending a bit more on their hair.

Or husbands may find the location of the salon handy, and find the shop front presentation appealing.

OAPs may want to look younger!

See... just because you have your avatar in mind, doesn't mean only your avatar is going to buy from you.

BUT REMEMBER... your avatar is important.

For all the reasons we said earlier – your avatar helps you make better marketing decisions. But also they become your raving fans.

If you can focus your business to serve one type of person, and serve them as best as you can – they will talk about you because you become remarkable to them, and word of mouth (and that indescribable buzz) will spread...

So, know your avatar inside out. It often helps if you give your avatar a name, a job, location, and even a face! Your avatar could even be a real person. Your avatar has very specific needs, and buys from you because of your brand values. You need to give your avatar a name, and constantly ask yourself "What would *name* want?" The name gives meaning and helps you to think of your real-life client's wants and needs.

One of the best avatars that we have ever heard of is a gym instructor who only works with 'nerds'. Brilliant Stand Out example!

Your Archenemy - who is your competition?

As well as knowing who you do want to work with, it can also be useful to sit down and think about the types of people you DON'T want to work with, and develop your archenemy to cater to these people.

Here's the thing about being a STAND OUT brand, you need to welcome people not liking you and not understanding you.

And you need to be 100% cool with that.

We know some people won't get this book, and what we believe in. In fact, did you know that the bestselling books on Amazon also have the highest proportion of 1 star reviews?

Don't be afraid of being Marmite! As Taylor Swift says, "Haters gonna hate" so don't worry about the people who aren't interested in your offering. Don't be offended by people who don't like what you do - take it is a compliment and move on. Remember: indifference is the death of Stand Out.

Having haters is a good sign, because it means that what you're doing is different enough for people to have an opinion. If you look at any big, successful brand, they all have people who don't like them.

Some people detest Apple and what they stand for, but more people love what they do.

This happens in business in the same way as it does in popular culture. Justin Bieber, Lady Gaga, Obama, One Direction, Manchester United. All hugely successful, but all with their fair share of haters.

So what to do with this?

Now you have embraced your haters, create an arch-nemesis. An arch-nemesis is your competitor with the opposite brand values to you. Every time you prepare to do something new, you should ask yourself: "Would my archenemy do this? Or would they do it better?" If the answer is yes, don't do it.

When we started out in business creating websites, our archenemy was bedroom coders or big agencies. There are some web developers we love, but unfortunately many have a bad reputation, so we wanted to be the anti-web developers, who could use our graphic design super-powers to create sites that looked awesome for small businesses who wanted to look the business. People loved that, and we got so many people telling us we 'weren't like other web designers'. Awesome!

Invest, Don't Struggle

The two reasons people don't invest in their brand are:

1) It's effort, and
2) It costs.

That shouldn't matter!

We would strongly recommend you invest in your branding. As we said earlier, branding is everything you do, the gut feeling you want your potential customers to feel. You can't just skimp on that or hope for the best. We aren't just talking about investing in a logo, but invest some time into thinking about the image you want to portray, the types of customers you want to attract and where you want your business to go. Obviously design work plays a large part in portraying all this also, and it is the one thing we see businesses fail to invest in. Here are three reasons why it's worth making that investment:

1. You want to compete. In many ways business is like a competitive sport, you want to be one step in front of the competition and you want people to support you (i.e. buy from you!). Not having a strong brand at the beginning is automatically giving yourself a handicap

At the very beginning of your business you need to catch up when it comes to looking credible and branding can help that massively. If you want to compete then having the right image is vital. Don't pretend you have been going for ages (dishonesty and branding don't mix), but having a suitable brand image that gives you the credibility to compete is vital. And it doesn't have to be too expensive. In fact don't think of it as an expense; think of it as an investment to get greater returns.

2. You understand your business a lot better. When you start a business it is easy to try everything once and see what sticks; however, this isn't the most effective way to grow your business. Having a greater understanding of your brand means you can target and specialise, and then execute more effective marketing strategies. It will help you make decisions about where your business is going in the future, allow you to communicate more effectively with your customers, and help you give a better service too.

3. It is easier than changing down the line. A lot of people start with something basic with the aim to invest more into their brand when their business is growing. There are a couple of issues there. One – your business will grow much quicker if you invest in branding (due to points 1 and 2). Two – getting it right at the beginning saves time and effort later on. Let's just look at the extreme basics of branding from a design point of view – logo, business name, business cards (there is so much more to it than this).

If you have those basics in place at the start and then build your business, when the time comes to move to the next level, people will already be familiar with your existing logo, domain name and email and it can be expensive and time-consuming to change everything. It is doable, but getting it right at the beginning can actually save masses of time and money later on!

Here's why these three reasons work...

We had a client who sold a premium £5,000 programme to CEOs. After a year of struggling to sell not even one spot on the package she came to us. The programme was sound, but the branding was not, the wording, tone and design of the brochure she had done herself on Microsoft Word and the web page didn't scream £5,000 either. We reflected and improved the wording, invested in high quality (but not cheesy) photography, and made a luxurious landing page with a download for her brand new shiny eBrochure.

This cost her less than £2,000 but after just a few weeks she sold out of all six spaces left on her programme making her £30,000 (all up front, may we add). So when we say branding and design is an investment - it is! Spending £2,000 made her £30,000.

Why did this work?

Well it's because we looked at her brand values and then looked at her target market, and adjusted accordingly.

We altered the language to sound like a more high-end item for aspiring CEOs, calling it 'Programme' rather than 'Package' or 'Course' makes it sound better and more certified.

We made it exclusive to only six people rather than trying to just get as many as possible. Six people was around the limit anyway so why not make it exclusive? It sounds better and more in line with the target buyers. They are top of their game, they don't want something anyone can get. It also got them to buy quicker as they didn't want to miss out.

The design looked the bomb! And why wouldn't it?! You're paying £5,000 - it should look mint!

The images we used showed the benefits of the programme, of being number one and having the support of your team behind you.

The fact that you had to enter a lot of details in to download the brochure positioned the programme very well. It suggests that it is so high value that it must be worth putting in all this info just to get a brochure. That it isn't for everyone, it is for 'me'. It almost pre-qualifies them. It gets them to put their hand up. And afterwards our client could give them a call to meet and to seal the deal.

The fact is that nothing had changed in the way the programme was being advertised other than changing and improving the design and tone to match the brand and to match the customer's expectations. Our point is that the time is now to invest in your brand to ensure it aligns to your brand values and speaks to your avatar.

We're about to get to the assignment in a moment which will help you to think more effectively about your brand to make it clear, but what about costs of design work? If you really can't invest in design then our Graduation Pack includes full step-by-step guides on how to fake being a designer, what tools to use that are free or ridiculously inexpensive and lots of other cool stuff. Claim your Graduation Pack here: www.thehippocampusbook.com

ASSIGNMENT

Now you have read this module, we want you to fully craft your own brand, to give yourself your own framework for thinking creatively. Here's a recap of the tasks needed to be completed:

Task 1: Get a blank piece of paper, and write down as many brand values that you can think of that relate to your company. You could think of these as 'how you would like people to describe your company when you are out of the room.' There isn't a right or wrong amount here. You may have in mind exactly how you want to be perceived, or you may at this point just be exploring your options. Just get creative for now. In the Graduation Pack there is a big, long list of possible brand values if you need some inspiration.

Task 2: From your list decide on the words that you think the majority of your competitors, or other businesses in your industry, would also use to describe themselves. Cross these out, or put them to one side. These are your 'Baseline Values'. Yes - these are important to live up to, but you can't build a Stand Out brand based on values that are the norm in your industry. If you end up crossing all your values out, you need to start again from Task 1, and dig a little deeper into what really makes you special.

Task 3: The remaining values should be 'Stand Out' values. From these, group similar values together and for the group decide upon a 'Headline Stand Out Value' for each group. You should be aiming for 3-5 Stand Out Values in total. If you have more than this, then you need to decide which 5 you think represent your business the best.

There you have it - your values are created. This is a really important step to do, as like we said this gives you your framework for thinking creatively. Without these values at hand, it will be hard to be confident that you are making the right marketing decisions.

Task 4: Craft your avatar. It is really important we know who our ideal customer is. The one perfect person who can become a raving fan of our business and help spread the word. Decide who your avatar is now, and 'flesh out' this character. Avatars do tend to be fictional, but if you have a real life avatar, that's fine too. You should know your avatar's: name, age, job, their pain points, their desires, where they like to hang out…

Task 5: Decide on your archenemy. This is the competition that you don't ever want to be like. By defining who you aren't - you define who you are. When we were web designers we said to people that we were the anti-web designers, because typically web designers have a bad reputation for being unreliable, ripping people off and being hard to get in touch with. This is not only great to say that you are the opposite of, but also gives you ideas for your business of how to Stand Out. For example, we found that most web developers/designers stereotypically take ages to get back to you via email, so we said that all emails from clients would be responded to within 24 hours if not less. Our clients loved this and raved about us to everyone they know. We still get referrals to this day for websites, from customers over 4-5 years ago.

So who is your archenemy? Write it down. It doesn't have to be one person or company, it can also be a set of characteristics or even stereotypes.

Final point: By doing these tasks in the past for ourselves, we were really able to shape and define our offering, and create a business that really resonated with our audience. Because we did this from the beginning, we got initial traction quicker, but it doesn't mean you have to stick with it forever.

Our brand has developed with our business, as our experience grew and we worked out what we wanted our business to look like. Your stereotypical web designer isn't our archenemy any more. At the time of writing this our archenemy is marketing companies who want to work with 'corporate clients' on broadcast messages. That doesn't resonate with us or our clients, as our aim is to help our clients do what other marketers won't have the balls to do. So you can see how this helps clearly define your audience and helps them to decide in a split second whether they like you or not.

When you've completed these tasks, you'll now have an understanding of what you are, what you stand for, who you want to work with and who you don't want to work with.

Every time you have to make a decision, you can ask yourself, "What would *my avatar* want?" and, "Does this align to my Brand Values?"

As we go onto Module 3, this will also give you a framework to run ideas through. You don't have to be afraid of Stand Out Marketing ideas as long as they are on-brand, and will resonate with your avatar.

SOM103:
Making Your Business Stand Out

In this section, we'll be sharing some practical ideas on how you go about making your business Stand Out against the competition.

You've already looked at why Standing Out is important, and laid the foundations of a Stand Out way of life, with a solid brand to make sure you make the right decisions for your Stand Out Marketing. Now it's time to fuel it, to help you spark awesome ideas, get creative, and get your business noticed, remembered and talked about.

Now you've worked through the exercises in the earlier sections, you'll have developed a Stand Out mind-set. Are you excited to put this into action!? Remember, being Stand Out is not about buying lots of things or being ridiculous, it's more about what money can't buy - thinking creatively, and that's what we're going to push you towards.

There are two ways to be different and Stand Out: you can either be 'better', or 'remarkable'.

Here's the distinction: if you are better, people will talk about how good you are when prompted to talk about your company or the industry in general - e.g. if somebody gets asked if they know of anybody who does what you do.

This is great, but what we really want to do is Stand Out in a remarkable way, and get people talking about us without being prompted.

We are going to go into being remarkable in a lot more detail, but first let's look at being 'better', as there is still great value in this.

How to be Better

You need to build on not just your product or service, but also your marketing and everything you do around your business. If you improve on what you're doing, people will recommend you when asked about your industry. For example we get asked all the time, "Hey do you know any good web designers"? The only two we could recommend are those who have given us excellent customer service, are reliable, and get the job done quickly. Given the reputation of many web designers, this is a massive improvement and the reason we are recommending them. They have impressed us and we know we can rely on them, so we will suggest them over anyone else.

The goal is to be better than your competition, in any way you can. The winners are those who are better in ways that the customer (your avatar) actually cares about.

In this example, 'better' just means a more reliable service in an industry lacking reliability. Something like, "Did you hear about the company who can build you a website in a day?!" - is also another great example of being better. And when the choice of who to buy from comes up, you're more likely to talk about and go with someone who is 'better'.

Being better is important, and being the best is the ultimate goal. If you are better than most, your word of mouth referrals will be increased, your customers will become fans and you can get much more repeat business. Being the best means that you can dominate a market and benefit from the credibility it brings.

Here are a few things to look at when you want to make what you do better. Whilst reading them think about all your touchpoints: your customer service, response times, your emails, your adverts, your sales funnels, your product, your invoicing, your business cards, your production process, the end results you give your consumers and so on:

1. *Speed*

Speed impresses like hell! The quicker you can be at responding, completing a task or improving customer service, the better. We live in a fast world where people expect things instantly and complain if they don't get it. Customer service studies have found that people can get pissed off if they don't get a reply within eight hours, or more often within a shorter timeframe.

Try to speed up everything, go the extra mile and make it seem like it's not an effort. We used to say that we'd reply to emails within 24 hours, because our archenemy (web developers) rarely get back to customers that quickly, if at all. It's not good if people have to wait weeks for a reply, so our guarantee was that we'd respond quickly, which impressed a lot of people.

What we were doing was leveraging what we had – as a start-up we had an abundance of time, so were able to offer a quick turnaround. It wouldn't be quite so easy for us to do that today. However, we will stay late to make sure someone gets a reply that little bit quicker. Look at what you have an abundance of, and use it.

You need to give the impression that this hasn't been laboured or an effort, or that you expect anything in return. You don't want to complain that you've been put out or draw attention to what you did in a "look at me" way.

Also, in some businesses it can be nice to show that you appreciate other people's time, as this creates brand loyalty. For instance, the Frankie and Benny's near our office do a guaranteed 40-minute lunch, which shows that they know how busy business owners are. Smaller cafes can struggle with this because they can't serve people quite as quickly.

Think about your industry and the processes you must all do, is there a way of improving the speed of what you can deliver (without reducing quality)?

Can you make your online tool work quicker than everyone else? Can your programme get results quicker than others?

Look at your processes – anything you do more than once means that you can create a process and speed it up, or outsource it so that it doesn't eat into your time.

Time - or the lack of - is something we bet 99% of consumers struggle with - we can use that!

2. *Frequency – Multiply the Recommended*

Marketing people always recommend doing a task so many times, such as attend a certain number of networking events each month, write so many blog posts a week, or Tweet so many times a day.

Eight Tweets a day is what we often hear recommended, however, because that is advised, doesn't that make you the same as most people? Kim Garst Tweets over a hundred times a day. You might think that's too much but actually Twitter is so fast paced, if you're only Tweeting eight times or fewer a day your visibility and engagement with your Tweets is going to be minor. By Tweeting so avidly, Kim ensures she gets seen every day when people are browsing their feed. More exposure means more engagement, trust, and sales.

Don't annoy people, but increase the regularity with which you do things. For instance, if you meet with clients once a quarter, could you increase that to once a month, or once a week?

Another good example is when you ask a company to do you a logo design. Designers usually give you three concepts to look at, choose the one you like and have up to three alterations. But that's rubbish! They might get it horribly wrong and then you're stuck with it and don't want to spend more money.

When we did logo design, we always offered unlimited revisions, because we want the customer to be happy. The other designers were our archenemy, and we didn't want to restrict customers to how many changes they could have, because your brand is one of the most important parts of your business. This was really popular and most of the time we only had to make a couple of revisions anyway. The rare occasions where we did lots of revisions, the customer was delighted with the end result and told everyone.

This showed confidence in our abilities and made a statement that we would offer unlimited revisions but there was no risk for us as we were confident we could get it right after 1 or 2 revisions. Everybody is a winner.

Think about what you do and what you offer, and what could you "up" (increase)?

When John Lee Dumas started a daily podcast, most people told him it was impossible to keep up, but actually it just shortened his time until success. In just two years he was making anywhere between $100,000 - $500,000 each month. If he had done a weekly podcast that same success might have taken him 14 years!

3. *Quality*
Having an awesome product or service is a great way to Stand Out.

Remember, treat business like an Olympic sport. You need to have the highest quality you possibly can to survive. The better the quality, the more referrals and praise you will receive.

Whatever you do, do it the best possible way you can!

One way to improve quality is through self-development - we never stop learning. Be a Terminator when it comes to self-development – never stop!

> "Be a Terminator when it comes to self development - *never stop*."
>
> thehippocampusbook.com
> by @andrewandpete

Don't get complacent and don't become stale (we'll touch on this again a little later). Always bring your top game. Always try to stay on top of industry trends, new and improved sources of inspiration or raw materials, always keep reading about new subjects, testing new things.

In Seth Godin's book *What to do When it's Your Turn* he talks about a farmer in Kenya called Lucy, who is the richest farmer in all of the villages close by. Her kids go to private school and she has a nice car. The only thing that she does differently to the other farmers is try new methods of growing her crops. If it doesn't work then no bother, just a little test. But if it does work, then she has found a way to be better than her competitors. The other farmers in the area were too afraid to try anything new for risk of failing. It is the constant testing of new ideas that has made her rich; the same goes for you.

When it comes to your marketing materials, beautifully designed items always Stand Out, so it's worth investing in these. In a lot of markets sole traders don't make these investments, which makes them look unprofessional or even scammy. Good quality materials and designs gives the appearance of excellent products or services, and also makes a company appear successful if they can afford better marketing materials. Success attracts success.

Another example of great quality comes from Social Media Marketing World (SMMW), which we attended in San Diego. It was really well planned out and made for an indescribably awesome experience! Every touchpoint was maximised, and in the lead up to the event they promoted the idea that no-one should get to SMMW and not know anyone. As you can imagine, the social media around the event was exceedingly good, connections were made beforehand so that when attendees arrived nobody felt alone. As you walked around you bumped into people you'd met online.

The world's leading experts were there, and there were 130 in total, far more than any other conference of its type, and everything was so organised. They had 100 staff on hand just to help you out, and there was even a hashtag to tweet for assistance. All the sessions were arranged to allow delegates to make the most of it and they were all recorded with slides, so you could watch it again later or catch up with a session you missed.

The catering was also organised so that 3,000 people weren't queuing for hours. The dining area was divided up so that people got their food quickly and sat in a small group, and there was a lunchbox system to make the midday meal easier. Another nice touch was the "community" sections where each table had its own different topic of conversation, so that people in the same industry – bloggers, podcasters etc. – could get together and share ideas over their food.

But even small businesses can deliver good quality. When we got our headshot photos taken, we wanted to look like we'd exploded. We took the concept to our photographer - Laura Pearman - and she told us exactly what we needed and how to do it, and the results were awesome. So many people comment on them and we always credit Laura because they make us Stand Out. She was 'better' than everyone else because she got our creative style and knew exactly how to get the photos we were after, and made it as easy as possible for us to achieve the look we wanted.

4. *Be More Useful*
Salesy doesn't sell!

> Take a photo of this and Tweet using #hippocampusbook
>
> "SALESY *DOESN'T* SELL."
>
> thehippocampusbook.com
> by @andrewandpete

People don't need more sales messages, but they do need their lives to be made easier. Make your marketing more useful and your business more useful and make everything less painful, from the process of buying online, to using your product and so on.

A big trend at the moment is content marketing, which is all about producing useful or interesting content – the pull rather than the push. If you're helping people out you pull them in and it gives meaning to your marketing. This helps build trust and credibility and stronger relationships, so that when that person is ready to buy they come to you.

The market has almost become saturated, so there is a lot of emphasis on producing better content and how people consume it – podcasting and video are very popular the moment. People are also double and triple screening, which means they are looking at their smartphones at the same time as browsing on their computer and watching TV. To be successful, you need to capture and hold their attention with useful content. Facebook algorithm changes basically mean that your posts won't get seen unless they are amazingly useful content that people engage with (otherwise you need to pay to get reach). The world doesn't need more content, but it does want better content. If your blog is the best blog on that topic then it will get noticed, shared and spread around. Maybe make your aim to do fewer blogs, but make these amazing. Use multimedia, embed graphics, sound bites, infographics, slideshows, GIFs, videos, Tweetables, links to further reading, find or conduct extra research to support your arguments, go really in depth, include interviews and quotes of other industry leaders. Think about your last blog, did it include any of them? Enough of them to Stand Out?

Go the extra mile to help people. If it is easiest to learn from your site consistently, then you will Stand Out.

5. *Niche*
Have you ever heard the statement, 'The riches are in the niches'. It only works if you say 'niche' like the Americans say it, haha!

However the point remains, industry leaders Stand Out. If you are the best in the world or in your area, then that is super impressive and it Stands Out. It's tough to be the best at something broad like say social media... but you could be the best in the world at say Facebook Ads - just one niche section of social media. The smaller the niche the less competition. For example, if you wanted to build a membership site, who would you rather go to, the web designer who builds any website, or the web designer who only specialises in membership sites? The choice is obvious, the second guy. The more you niche down, the more focused you are on that niche and thus the better you will be at it. Or at least that is the perception!

Most people come to the conclusion that niching down limits your audience size too much, but there are 7 billion people in the world, and most have

Internet access - the niche can almost never be too small. Believe us.

When it comes to generating referrals then, who is going to Stand Out the most when someone starts talking about a membership site? The second guy. If anyone talks about membership sites, then his name will come up.

Is it enough to just be better though?

Looking at the Discus Model, you will find that being better only gets you so far.

It's all well and good to improve yourself in the ways we've outlined, but let's take it a step further! You need to be different and you need to get people talking about you without being prompted. As we said, being better means you're recommended, but when you're remarkable people talk about you unprompted. The guy who does membership sites might be the one who Stands Out and gets talked about when we're discussing website designers for memberships sites, but we're not going to go to our friends and business contacts and talk all day about him, nor post about him on social media sites.

How to Be Remarkable

Like we said, to be remarkable doesn't just mean being really good, or great, even amazing - no, it means worth making a remark about.

It means being different enough to Stand Out in such a way that people just have to stop, watch, appreciate and most importantly, tell others.

And this is crucial.

This is how you are going to get talked about, as well as noticed and remembered. If you can get word of mouth to spread the news about your company without people needing to be prompted then you are onto a winner!

BETTER VS. REMARKABLE TABLE

	GET NOTICED	GET REMEMBERED	GET TALKED ABOUT
BETTER	You will get noticed if looking	You will be remembered until someone better comes along	You will be talked about when prompted and in the right context
REMARKABLE	You will get noticed whether looking or not	You will be remembered indefinitely and achieve top of mind awareness	You will be talked about unprompted

As you can see in this table, although being better does get you noticed, remembered and talked about, the difference when you are remarkable is clear... when you can catch people's attention who aren't necessarily looking, you achieve true Top of Mind Awareness indefinitely rather than until something better comes along, and you are talked about not just when your subject/industry is brought up, but rather people will talk about you unprompted.

All of which inevitably leads to more sales.

Rich Schefren has a great example for differentiation and remarkability that perfectly sums up our point and had us in stitches. We've paraphrased a little here...

"Consider this, at some point in your life you will have been to the best public toilet that you have ever been to.

Do you go telling everyone about it? No, it's just a toilet.

Besides, you might come across weird if you talk about it to people anyway.

However, imagine if you went into the toilets, gentlemen, and saw this:

How funny is that, a graphic of a woman looking down at your... ahem."

Anyway, it's remarkable and you are going to go back in the bar, or maybe home that night and tell people about it, you may even take a pic (as long as nobody is around) and post it on Facebook. Suddenly you're not weird anymore, suddenly it makes you interesting that you know about it, and that makes others want to check it out too so they can see for themselves and tell their friends.

So then being remarkable isn't just about being different, but rather different in a way that creates a talking point. It makes people want to talk about you.

Let us give you another example. How many stationery companies are there? The majority of them are pretty much the same and selling the same branded goods. They can however make themselves better by promising things like next day delivery, having a smooth ordering system, great customer service, ever expanding catalogue etc. All great strategies for keeping customers happy, but does it get them talking?

When we first moved to the North East, there was one stationery company that completely got our attention. It is called TLC Office Supplies, and it offers stationery + free biscuits.

If you order some stationery over a certain amount from TLC not only do you get a great service (better) but also you receive a pack of biscuits through the post too. TLC plays on this so much to help them Stand Out. Tom, the company's owner is even called 'The Director of Biscuits'.

What a great way of creating a talking point! Tom has told us many times how he has managed to build up customer relationships with this strategy and keep that all important Top of Mind Awareness.

Moreover, you can imagine the following conversations or social media posts, 'Look what I got in the post today..."

Tom's business grew into a six figure beast off the back of this promotion, and it proves the point that being Stand Out
doesn't have to be complex or expensive.

With that said, how can you make people stop, stare and talk about you?

Getting that All-important Remarkability

There are two ways you can look at the word 'remarkable', in terms of getting that all-important remarkability factor.

1. Remarkability: Simply being different to the majority.

In a world full of more businesses than ever, every single industry has its norms. It has the things that everybody does because it is standard.

Most urinals have adverts at eye level.

Most designers take 50% upfront, 50% at the end.

Most shops have a queuing system to pay.

Most managed office spaces include free tea and coffee.

By highlighting your industry norms and switching lanes you can catch people off guard and when people come across anything unique… they talk about it.

Let's take one of those examples… *most managed office spaces include free tea and coffee.*

There came a time when we were in the market for a new office (let us tell you - that is an industry that could do with some remarkability). Then we came across Gateway House in Newburn Riverside.

Everything about it was 'better'. The customer service, the decor, the reception area, the added extras... then we got to the kitchen...

"Here's where we keep the tea and coffee that you can help yourself to. Oh and here is the beer fridge, we stock it full once a week, feel free to help yourself at any time."

What?!

Free coffee, tea... and beer. Now that's remarkable.

Can you imagine saying this at a networking event:

"How are you?"
"I'm great thanks, I've just moved office into a building, it's really nice, lovely wallpaper."

Probably not...

How about...

"How are you?"
"I'm great thanks, I've actually just moved office into a really cool building... it has a beer fridge."

That's more like it. See how remarkable trumps better.

Taking it back to the 'Discus Model', being different to the majority is certainly going to get us noticed, certainly going to get us remembered, and in some cases it will get us talked about. But what we really want to do is guarantee that we get talked about. That's the key in all this remember. That's the holy grail.

Remember 'Super Dogs' from earlier in this book? Things got interesting as soon as Iron Man developed a strategy to get people talking about him.

2. Remarkability: Getting people to talk about you.

Remarkable means 'worth making a remark about'. So not only must we switch lanes, and be different to the majority in our industry, we must also understand why and how people talk to other people.

All too often businesses want to be talked about, yet they either don't make it easy to talk about them, or they don't understand why people want to talk about what they do.

Newsflash: It is very rare for somebody to simply share something online and offline out of the goodness of their hearts. There are psychological reasons people share stuff.

Now, we aren't psychologists, we are marketers, but we can take note of the motivations people have for sharing things. We can do this in day to day life by paying attention to when a business contact gets shared, or somebody comes up in conversation, by simply asking ourselves...

'Why was that person prompted to bring up that business?'

Or another cool activity we can do is look down our social feeds at content that is being shared by people who didn't create it, and ask ourselves the same question...

'Why is that person sharing that?'

You can do this yourself even right now.

Top Tip: Especially take note of who is talking about your competition, and why are they talking about them.

It all Comes Down to Social Currency

With the rise of the Internet and the various social networks, we are living our lives now online. Though this also applies with how we interact offline, the online world has never been more important for businesses to master. Offline we can have people talking about us 1-1, or one to a small group, but online we can get people to broadcast our message whole audiences of hundreds and thousands of people in their network, all for FREE.

We would be stupid to ignore that.

But what we say and do defines us. Everything we share on our social networks are signals to the world saying who we are. What it means to be you. Are we team Apple or team Samsung? Are we into fitness? Are we doing anything this weekend, and what are our views on hot topics? It all defines us. The only reason then people will share something is because it speaks to their world view, and it helps to define them in the way they want to be defined.

So we as business owners should be looking to create messages and stories that people can share... that makes them look good and that adds to their social currency, not ours.

Here's quite an extensive (though not necessarily all-inclusive) list of why people talk/share things online and offline. When reading through this next part we want you to be asking yourself if the things you do are actually giving people a reason to talk about your business.

Emotion

Emotion has a big part to play in marketing. It is estimated buying decisions are 20% logic and 80% emotion, so it is safe to say emotion has a big part to play in getting people to talk about you too. Luckily we as human beings have a lot of emotions to play off!

Humour - We're going to go here first, because humour - if used correctly, simply WORKS. People talk about funny things, and share funny things because they get the credit, and they look like the funny one. If you have a brand that allows you to use humour to make people laugh, we would urge you to go for it.

People are scared of looking foolish, or being laughed at, but remember being Marmite is good and laughing at yourself is a fantastic way to humanise your business, make people trust you, and make them feel like they have a stronger connection with you. This is why cats trying to make a long jump from a sofa to an armchair does so well online (spoiler alert: they never make it), but our absolute favourite example of this for businesses is the 'Dollar

Shave Club' YouTube video that went viral a few years back. Go watch it if you can. It is a perfect example of how to use humour and get your core message across.

Humour can be one of the easiest and cheapest ways to catch attention, but it is also subjective - so make sure your avatar finds it funny.

Anger - On the opposite side of the scale, anger is another strong emotion you can use well in your marketing. Now with anger, you don't want people to get angry at your business, that would obviously be counter-productive, but if you can use anger with a happy ending, that's always a winner.

Bark Box, a subscription service of goodies for your dog, put together a video called 'Caitlyn's Best Day' which documented the story of Caitlyn the dog, who's had electrical tape tied around her mouth to act as a muzzle, eventually deforming her face. The video documented Caitlyn's rescue, rehabilitation and then her best day including chasing hundreds of tennis balls, getting the 'bone to the city', and then finally finding a new, loving, foster family. Family pets are always close to people's hearts so you can imagine the anger and emotion that the video must evoke, before Caitlyn is finally rescued. It's worth talking about, sharing, and all the good will generated goes to Bark Box.

Awe - Think of all the amazing things you see talked about online, from breath-taking views and experiences, to OMG moments. Can your marketing inspire awe? For example, we once booked to attend an event in Las Vegas, and saw somebody share a video online of a first person view of a zip wire through Vegas. Not just a zip line in the middle of nowhere though, right through a shopping centre with everyone around. We instantly re-shared this - how cool would it be to do this?! Great marketing for the company who runs the zip wire.

Shock - People do tend to stay away from shock due to the nature of the beast, and not wanting to offend. Though as long as you are staying away from discrimination and prejudice, it can be a great way to make a noise, and get people sharing your stuff. Just think of 99% of charity videos which show horrifying images you can't help but watch and may share online to help spread the cause.

If you aren't a charity though, there is another three letter word that sells - SEX. Kylie Minogue's Agent Provocateur advert was banned from being shown in cinemas, it was so shocking (it has made its way onto YouTube if you are curious), but what a talking point that was! Having a banned advert actually made the company even more of a talking point. Imagine if YouTube was more popular at that time, she would have broken the Internet long before Kim Kardashian and *that* Champagne bottle. If you can shock people, they will talk about it.

Sticking with pop stars, in 2013 Beyoncé shocked fans by releasing a surprise studio album on iTunes, complete with 17 new music videos. In the first three hours she sold a whopping 80,000 copies in the first three hours. The reason why this is so groundbreaking is because there was zero promotion - just the shock factor. If you were one of the first to know about it, you would tell others because it makes you look 'in the know'. Of course the media ate this up and the whole thing escalated in an extremely short space of time.

This worked for Beyoncé because the idea had never been done before on this scale in the music industry. What's never been attempted in your industry?

Annoyance - You have to ramp it up with this one. There's no point being mildly annoying, you will just be ignored. You have to be so annoying you go full circle back on yourself to become a talking point. If you live in the UK, you'll know what we mean with two words… "Go Compaaaaare!" We're cringing already.

Insurance comparison site Go Compare ran a TV campaign featuring a mad opera singer with a curly moustache who would sing the most irritating yet catchy 'Go Compare' tune in the most annoying Italian accent. It was voted the most irritating TV ads by Marketing Magazine for two years in a row and also made it to the top of the Metro's 'The top 20 adverts that Britain loves to hate'. To top it off the Facebook Group 'Go Compare, Go Compare, give me a bat to kill the t**t at Go Compare', has attracted 257,000 members - 50 times more followers than the TV commercials' official fan page!

A key phrase here though is 'love to hate'. We love to hate it because it gives us something to talk about and bond over, "OMG how annoying is that Go Compare guy?!". We can all be together on that common ground.

Moreover what's the first thing that comes to mind when you want to compare prices online and you're sitting in front of Google to type something in… Go Compaaaaare!

The result? Since running the ads, the company has gone from third in the market to first in a highly competitive market. Even more remarkable is the fact that it beat the Compare the Meerkat campaign from Compare the Market - an animated meerkat whose adverts have stolen the nation's hearts, spawned spin-off merchandise, and a best-selling autobiography.

We are personally team meerkat, but we aren't in the majority.

Sympathy/Empathy – Pete's brother John was doing 7 marathons for 7 days for charity, all dressed in a morphsuit. He was killing himself training after working 80 hours a week, but he wasn't generating any results in terms of donations. His Facebook page was only getting low reach and one or two likes per post, and after working hard for months he had only received £10. He was trying to do something amazing, and it seemed like people didn't care.

So we suggested he should lay all this out in a video and be completely transparent about how tough it is, how hard he was working, and what good the charity was doing. The video was shot naturally in a selfie style during training on a smartphone with no post-edit. It cost £0.

The results? The video picked up 10,000 views in two days, and he raised £1600 overnight. The video was then picked up by other media pages, and resulted in John getting sponsorship from Coors Light beer.

Why did this work? Because people share things they can sympathise or empathise with. There is a great power in being transparent and honest in business, as people will relate to you, and trust you more.

Admiration - A final emotion - admiration can be a big reason something is shared online. If people get to know you so much that they admire you, they will want to actively promote and share anything you do.

You could build up a loyal audience who knows 100% what you put out is worth sharing without even checking for themselves. A good example of this is sometimes our blogs sometimes get tweeted before we even tweet them ourselves, by people who have set up tools to auto-tweet new blogs we publish - how cool is that!

So how do you reach admiration? You need to be consistent to your brand and true to your avatar - that's it. Because the people you resonate with will over time come to admire you. We all have people we look up to - you should be aiming to be one of those people too.

Do you see how all these emotions act as a driver to get people to talk about your business and in some way increase people's social currency? They're saying they agree/disagree with you, and getting across how they want to appear

When it comes to emotion, extreme emotions are better, for example, something hilarious is going to get shared and talked about much more than something that merely makes you smile. Excitement trumps contentment, anger trumps sad, and so on. If you are going to use emotion, don't do it half-heartedly.

We understand though, tapping into people's emotions can be hard depending on your business, but luckily for you, it isn't the only reason people share content online. Why else do people talk about things?

To Look Interesting

Going back to Super Dogs, Iron Man got us to share our photo with The Avengers because it made us look interesting. We didn't share it to advertise Iron Man's hot dog stand. If you can make other people look interesting with your marketing, you are onto a winner. When we decided to officially launch *atomic* at the North East Expo (a large trade fair in our area) we rented a Crystal Maze style cyclone machine that people could get into. Blasts of air blew hundreds of foam balls around and you had to try to catch as many as possible. We got hundreds of social media notifications of people talking about it and sharing images of them or their friends in it, because it made them look interesting!

To Look Entertaining

It's not just funny videos that get shared, in fact if we can make our marketing remotely entertaining, the same principles apply... people share to look entertaining themselves. Some TV ads do this really well - just think Superbowl ads - but small businesses can do this with their content marketing as well. The camera on an iPhone (team Apple through and through), makes it possible for anybody to shoot HD videos and post them online, and now there's services like Facebook Live, Periscope and Blab that are bringing live video to the forefront. The last few years has seen the birth of 'YouTube Stars', some of whom either had a business, or made it a business because they were entertaining. Size doesn't matter. People share entertaining content from the big and the small.

To Massage Their Ego

This is a slightly different reason for people to share, but if you are a type of company that helps people accomplish something, creating content that helps them talk about their accomplishments - and therefore massage their ego - is a great way to get talked about. Weight Watchers is a great example of this - some of their groups have virtual certificates people can post to their Facebook page after losing so many pounds.

To be Useful

B2B blogging is a good example of this. People will share other people's blogs if they are helpful (not sales messages), so they look like somebody in the know. Though this is good, we are in a noisy world when it comes to blogging, so when we say 'be useful', we mean 'be remarkably useful'. A great example of a marketing campaign with great remarkability was from Nivea for Men, who developed their 'Life Hacks' campaign for busy men on the go. They put together a series of short life hacks like 'how to make a beer cold in 5 minutes' or 'how to reheat pizza without ruining it'. Really, really useful content that solves everyday problems for their avatar in a way that could be talked about and shared - "Hey have you seen this? Look what I can do…"

Because They're Sparked

This can work well, but it takes some serious brain power. If we think hard enough of ways to make our marketing fit in with everyday life, we can find clever ways to 'spark' people to talk about us constantly.

Remember that god-awful Rebecca Black song 'Friday'? Literally every time one of us said 'It's Friday' for months after, the other one would burst into song 'It's Friday, Friday, gotta get down on Friday, everybody's lookin' forward to the weekend, weekend.' We were sparked!

If someone says, "Have a break," do you automatically want to say back, 'Have a Kit Kat'? Again, it's sparked. Advertising has made you link up the two in your mind over time with repetition, and now one doesn't come without the other.

Can you link up your marketing messages to common words or phrases people say or things they do in order to have them thinking and talking about you constantly?

Because They're Forced

This is only applicable to some businesses, but you see it all the time on things like Facebook games.

'Share with your Friends to get more lives'. Not the right strategy for everybody for sure, but it can work.

Growth Hackers at Dropbox gave a great example of this when they needed to increase customer acquisition. They basically gave you a free account with limited space on it, and to get more space all you had to do was share it. Post on Twitter for more free storage, or get a friend to sign up and gain more free space.

The result? They are now one of the market leaders in online storage solutions.

They're Curious

In one of the Internet's first big marketing success stories, people were glued to their mice and monitors when The Blair Witch Project executed one of the most remarkable marketing campaigns on a budget. The film 'leaked' 'found footage' and the Internet went into meltdown debating whether it was real or not. Why did that work? Because people were just too damn curious.

Adele made her comeback in curiosity building circumstances in late 2015 too, releasing just a snippet of her new song out of the blue in an advert break. No announcement who it was by, just a familiar voice. Twitter blew up with curiosity as people talked about it. Again small businesses can build curiosity too in their campaigns and language used. When we launched *atomic*, we didn't just say 'HERE IT IS'. We teased it for months, building curiosity, then launched. We even had people sign up before they even knew what it was properly, just because they were so curious and wanted to be the first in the know.

The Extremity Scale - are we desensitised to all this?

Here's the crux of all this. We need to be remarkable enough in order to get the tongues wagging about us.

If the tongues aren't wagging we need to ramp up our game.

The more extreme we can be in any of these areas, the further we can get in the Discus Model from noticed, to remembered to talked about.

If we are only a little bit useful, funny or interesting then we aren't going to get very far.

Here's an example... where Andrew listens to podcasts more, Pete loves reading business books.

He reads a lot, and has an app on his phone that reads out key point summaries so he can 'read' even more books. But if a book is that useful, Andrew knows about it.

When Pete first read The 4 Hour Work Week by Tim Ferris he was blown away by its usefulness. He banged on about it for months, and it came up in many, many conversations. He bought Andrew a copy, and made his flatmate read it too. Its usefulness was remarkable. That doesn't happen with all books he reads - most of them are useful, but not remarkably useful.

In the earlier example of the Super Dogs, you would think that just being dressed up as Iron Man would do the trick, right? But not in this day and age. We've seen someone dressed as Iron Man in the street before; it's not that extreme. All day long we can watch extremely remarkable stories from our phone on YouTube, Facebook, Snapchat and so on. Things just don't impress us as much anymore.

This just makes our case for Standing Out even more important though; if you're average you have no chance.

Better, Remarkable, or Better and Remarkable?

We know there will be some of you reading this book saying that 'Actually I just want to be better. I don't need to be remarkable. I'm happy getting noticed and being remembered for my better service, and I'm getting enough word of mouth.'

To you we say, that's great... kind of.

Being better at what we do should definitely be in our strategies. We agree, there's no point in being remarkable and talked about if you can't come up with the goods afterwards. That could get you talked about for the wrong reasons.

But unless you are THE BEST, you are playing follow the leader, and although bettering your business is good, it is only going in one direction. You will never have the experience of change, or wanting to change, and one day you'll be forced to change.

Industries change, both big and small. Look how the advancements in technology have revolutionised many industries in the past 10 years, from music to marketing, to taxi services and even accountancy?

We love our accountants (shout-out to Dona and Andrew). When we signed up with them they were telling us about cloud accountancy, and the benefits of it, specifically the system they use called Xero.

That's awesome. They were getting ahead of the curve, because that's how we expected to do our accounts. The accounts industry had changed, and we definitely weren't going to get software that we had to manage from a desktop. We wanted to do our accounts on our iPhones.

However, we had a few other meetings with accountants who were still trying to sell us doing bookkeeping the old way. We wouldn't even consider that, and we doubt any new business (with founders under a certain age) setting up today would either.

Dona and Andrew changed how they did things to adapt because they were agile enough to do so. They could therefore make their business remarkably useful for us!

So to answer the question, to be a true Stand Out company, you need to be both better and remarkable.

Logistics of Sharing

Search for #atomicnetworking on Twitter and you will see lots of weird and wonderful selfies of business people in fancy dress! No, not because it is just way we do business in Newcastle, but rather because we have engineered it.

Everything about the event is better or remarkable including the first half hour of mingling where we encourage people to choose a selfie challenge at random from the 'Bowl of Destiny' (you have to say 'Bowl of Destiny' in a deep game show-esque voice to pull it off, haha!)

The challenges range from 'Take a selfie with someone you have never met before'… all the way to 'Take a selfie with someone and at the last minute stick your tongue out' or 'Bark like a dog' or, 'Choose from the fancy dress box with someone else and take a selfie together.'

It's just a fun little ice breaker but it does work! Not only does it get people talking to each other at the event but it has people talking about it after the event has taken place too.

We would have stopped there but we didn't. At the end of the challenge it states that you must also tweet the photo using the hashtag #atomicnetworking and there's a prize for the best one posted.

Now some of these photos are pretty odd and/or embarrassing. Surely these professional businessmen and women wouldn't share them online?

But they do!

Why do they do this? They do it because of what it says about them to post it online, it says: 'Hey, I'm not boring, I'm fun and look at me doing something interesting, don't you wish you were here too. I'm part of this great community.'

Did we stop there?

Nope. We also take a big group selfie shot at the end with everyone in (if they can fit!) using a selfie stick. From there we edit it into our brand colours, place our logo and networking details at the bottom and then send it out to everyone who came, encouraging them to share it - which they do.

That's why with no other promotion the group grows each and every time. It has a buzz about it.

People see how much fun others are having and want to part of the 'in' crowd too.

However, the point is, we designed it that way.

We thought about the concept of sharing in the planning phase of the event, not as an afterthought. This is what you should be doing too.

For example, the sole purpose of the initial Selfie Challenge was to get people talking about our event online. If 20 people have an audience of a few hundred/thousand each, word of the event will spread far and wide. We also didn't get people sharing something boring online either, the challenges were fun and created a talking point. Each photo shared created conversations from their followers and thus about our event.

We factored in time in the event schedule for the selfie challenges to take place and gave people an extra dedicated five minutes in the middle of the event, just in case they hadn't got around to it yet.

We gave them the props and selfie sticks to take photos with and helped out people who were struggling.

Finally, on the follow up email with the group selfie we also engineered shareability. Rather than hoping they would take five minutes out of their busy schedule to go through the laborious tasks of right click > save as > choose folder > rename it > save, then go to Twitter (and not get distracted) > click new

Tweet > write a Tweet, and hope they remember the right hashtags and say something nice - which is pure effort - instead we used a simple tool called Click to Tweet to effortlessly do it all for them. All they have to do is click and it will come up with a pre-written Tweet including the attached photo, with all the right hashtags.

Boom! That Easy.

If you would like to know how to do the Click to Tweet with a photo, as it can be tricky, it will be in your Graduation Pack (www.thehippocampusbook.com).

- Is it easy to share your product / event / service / marketing / content?
- How can you encourage people to talk about you online and make it easy for them?
- Are your main messages short and punchy enough to be easily remembered?
- Can you create photo opportunities?
- Can you use alliteration or rhyming words, or avoid jargon?

This is a crucial part that people miss. If you want people to talk about you and share stuff about you then you have to make it as easy as possible.

ASSIGNMENT

Right, are you ready?! This is probably the most crucial part of this book, as this is how you actually think of new Stand Out ideas. These tasks are what we use ourselves in our own business, when trying to think of original ideas, and are what we use with our clients too.

Task 1: We'll start you off easy. All we want you to do first is think about all your touchpoints. A touchpoint is any instance where your business communicates with somebody else in any way (verbal, visual or otherwise). From your business cards, your website, your receptionist and so on. We want you to make a list of all the touchpoints you can think of. We are big fans of pen and paper brainstorming, but unless you have a BIG piece of paper, this may be easier on a spreadsheet, there's a template in the Graduation Pack (www.thehippocampusbook.com).

Start with the boring.
As you are thinking of these touchpoints, a good idea is to what we call: start with the boring. 'The boring' are parts of your business which are standard across the industry. Things like: business cards, proposals, free consultation, packaging, thank you pages, voicemails, networking pitches. The great thing about

the boring touchpoint is that nobody expects them to be anything but boring! So if we can enhance our brand in a Stand Out way on the boring touchpoints, you get subconscious bonus points!

Task 2: Now, you can get to work thinking of new ideas. So take your brand values, that you created earlier on and put them in a table with your touchpoints like this:

BRAND MAXIMISER TABLE

Brand Maximiser	WEBSITE	BUSINESS CARDS	TWEETS	PROPOSALS	NETWORKING PITCH
STYLISH	Blogs about interior design trends, using beautiful photography. Lots of images.	Fill out the full table, thinking about how your touchpoints maximise your brand values.			
AMBITIOUS	Shares his vision for his company in a SlideShare presentation, displays awards he has won.	Fill out the full table, thinking about how your touchpoints maximise your brand values.			
PERSONABLE	A detailed about page with face to camera video, sharing his story. Light-hearted tone throughout.	Fill out the full table, thinking about how your touchpoints maximise your brand values.			
HASSLE FREE	Navigation of site is clutter free. Mobile friendly, fast loading. Prices are transparent.	Fill out the full table, thinking about how your touchpoints maximise your brand values.			
CUSTOMER DELIGHT	On every page there is a video of a happy customer giving a testimonial. Plus guarentees.	Fill out the full table, thinking about how your touchpoints maximise your brand values.			

[NOTE: See a larger image of this in the graduation pack]

Think of each touchpoint as a 'Brand Maximiser': these are the opportunities to maximise how people perceive you, and attract the right sort of person to you!

This is an example of an electrician's brand maximiser table (note: the list of touchpoints here is far from extensive). But let's take the first column: his website, see how we can match the aspects of his website to his brand values, to ensure he is getting across the right things. Some of these will be stronger than others.

Let's take 'Stylish' as an example.

You probably wouldn't describe the average electrician as 'Stylish', but this electrician is different. He wants to work with people who have an interest in interior design, and who need an electrician to install fashionable lighting, so you can see how he wants to get this across on his website (a big touchpoint), by using beautiful photography instead of the traditional stock photos you see on a lot of electricians' websites. Is this going to put off people who just want a new light put in? - sure, but that is fine!

Again it is crucial to note at this point, ideas should come from the brand values. If this electrician really wanted to be noticed, he could be dressed in a mankini wrestling a sumo wrestler on his Home Page. That would get noticed, that would get remembered, but it is crazy for the sake of it, not in line with his values. If one of his values was 'Random', 'Crazy' or 'Downright weird' that might work!

Now it is your go... look at all your touchpoints and ask yourself if they get across your brand values, if not, how could you improve them to do so? Remember start with the boring, and work through.

Task 3: Better or Remarkable. Now in an ideal world, it would be good to run every single touchpoint through this next task, but the reality of the amount of time you would have to dedicate to this would be epic. Instead pick some of the touchpoints you think are really important, and look at making them remarkable.

Note: This works for improving existing touchpoints, but we also use it now every single time we introduce a new touchpoint into our business.

BRAINSTORM TABLE

Uniform	STYLISH	AMBITIOUS	PERSONABLE	HASSLE FREE	CUSTOMER DELIGHT
BETTER	Clean uniform, with booties				
REMARKABLE	Tuxedo uniform!				

[NOTE: See a larger image of this in the graduation pack]

We take one of our touchpoints and put it in the top left corner, with the values this time running across the top. Then, using the better vs remarkable analogy as explained in this module, we think of ways that our touchpoint can not only be better (and therefore, get noticed and get remembered), but actually be talked about to. This above example looks at our electrician again, taking into account the uniform, how does our electrician look 'Stylish' in this case? To be better would be to have a clean uniform, and he might put on a pair of those throw away plastic booties before going into your house to avoid getting mud everywhere.

That's nice, but you wouldn't go around saying:

"My electrician had clean overalls on today," would you!?

How about if he turned up in a tuxedo? Or overalls that looked like a tuxedo?

That's an interesting story to tell somebody! Paraphrasing here, you could imagine somebody saying....

"I'm getting my house re-done, with these trendy new lights my electrician recommended, he knows his stuff... and you should have seen what he was wearing..."

A great example we used were our business cards. One of our values is Rule Breakers: We want to bend the rules of how things tend to be done, and stand out.

We looked at our business cards, and thought 'OK, how do we make these in line with our brand.'

We could have made them better, used our photography of us blown up to get attention, people may have even shared that. But we wanted to take it a step further.

We thought: 'We want to teach people how to do Stand Out Marketing, what if our business card literally stands out.' And so we created a pop-up business card, that you can actually pop open and stand up.

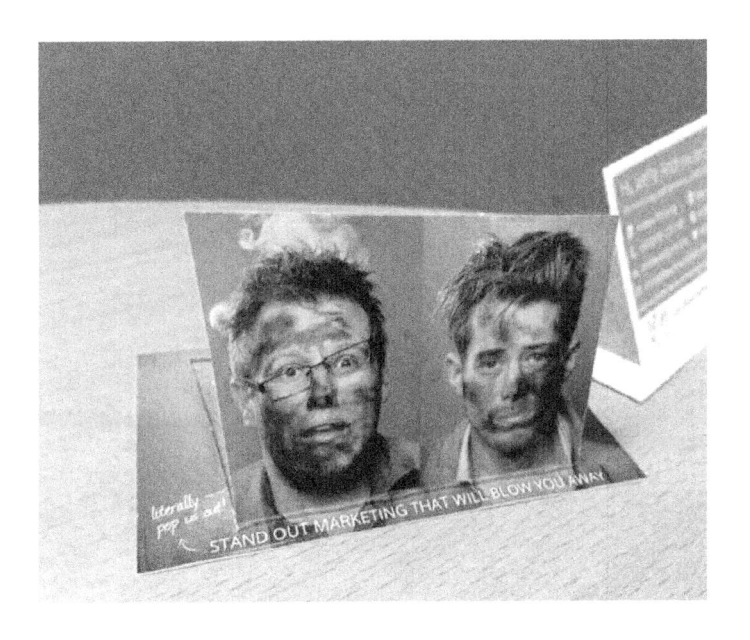

These were remarkable. People loved them, people shared them. People asked if they could take 2 so they could pass one on! Now that's getting talked about.

So now it is your turn. These ideas came because we planned them to be shareable. What aspects of your business are remarkable? Create your own better vs remarkable table and run 5 touchpoints through it, to see what you come up with.

SOM 104:
Inspiration

Now you should know: the importance of Standing Out, how to make the right Stand Out decisions by fully understanding your brand, and then how to make Stand Out decisions by thinking in a better and remarkable way. This section is about how to implement your new ideas and keep everything moving in the right direction.

Often, when people read a blog or a book they'll feel inspired to do something about it, but never do.

Do not be that person!

We're here to help you change your mind-set and give you the processes, as well as some tasks and challenges to ensure that you *do* do something about your business and take a step up. The last thing we want you to do when you finish this book is to think "That was a great idea" but then take no action.

You need to keep the momentum going.

Businesses with momentum naturally Stand Out, are more creative, and find time to be awesome.

4 Things you Need to Have in Place

To keep the momentum going and to be truly remarkable, you can't be different for just a day.

> Take a photo of this and Tweet using #hippocampusbook

> "To be *truly remarkable*, you can't be different for just a day."
>
> thehippocampusbook.com
> by @andrewandpete

You need to be constantly stretching your comfort zone. A lot of people get comfortable with their problems. They may only be making a certain amount of money, but get used to it rather than doing something about it. Or they may not get around to those website updates that need doing, despite the site generating no leads and leaking money.

To keep yourself away from that trap, and to continue Standing Out you need to treat your business like an Olympic sport. You are competing against the world so you need to constantly self-develop, constantly seek new ideas to stay fresh, and use all the support you can muster.

This needs to be taken seriously and won't just happen accidentally.

So here are four things to have in place.

1. A Place to Capture Slow Hunches

History has a way of defining huge breakthroughs in single momentous 'Eureka' moments - it just makes for a better story. Archimedes sitting in a bath and coming up with the theory of displacement, an apple falling on Newton's head and coming up with the theory of gravity, history is full of these moments.

The problem is that they are just stories. In reality these miraculous discoveries are actually ideas that Archimedes and Newton had been working on for some time. Years in fact.

If they hadn't had these ideas fixed in their subconscious mind already, and hadn't spent years trying to work it out, and if they hadn't dedicated their lives already to science, they wouldn't have come up with their idea in their eureka moment.

It's the same for you. A brilliant idea or breakthrough moment usually starts off as a small idea, niggling away until one day you crack it!

But how many ideas have you had and just discarded?

Maybe you thought they were a bit too 'out there' or just wouldn't work, or were too ambitious.

But what if they were actually life changing, amazing ideas that just needed a slight tweak?

What if they just needed a bit of time to develop?

This is called a slow hunch.

One of the best things we ever did was start to capture all our ideas whenever we had them. In this day and age our attention span is tiny and ideas are easily forgotten. Once written down, we can come back to them and develop them to see if they are actually worth pursuing. This has paid off for us massively! In fact, all of our big achievements have come about like this, starting off as just ideas worthy of dismissing, but instead we wrote them down and thought about them subconsciously and consciously till they developed into something workable.

Imagine if we had just forgotten about them. Yikes! You wouldn't be reading this book!

Imagine if the one thing that could dramatically change your life and your business was just an idea that you dismissed and forgot about. Scary right?

So step one is to write all your ideas down! The good, the bad, and the ugly. How you do this is up to you: some people prefer to carry around a notepad especially for ideas, or maybe you use something like Evernote, or maybe you just simply use an app on your phone like 'Reminders'. You could even use the voice recorder on your phone with a short description as the title.

Whatever you choose, from here on in make it a habit to write down ideas that come to you - no matter where you are! Oftentimes our best ideas come to us when we are not at work. Don't use that as an excuse, still capture those ideas. Use Siri if you have to: "Hey Siri, add to reminders…"

Challenge: We challenge you to write down at least five ideas that will help your business each day for the next month, just to get you going and into the habit.

Remember when it comes to ideas, quantity leads to quality.

Take a photo of this and Tweet using #hippocampusbook

"WHEN IT COMES TO IDEAS, *QUANTITY LEADS TO QUALITY.*"

thehippocampusbook.com
by @andrewandpete

You will have heard the phrase, "The fastest way to succeed is to fail more than anyone else". Well it's the same with ideas, and to Stand Out you need to be thinking creatively and come up with lots of ideas that help to make you better or remarkable.

Even if you don't think of yourself as particularly creative, everyone has the ability to get creative and think a bit differently. So don't worry or use that as an excuse, just get capturing ideas.

But what turns random ideas into great eureka moments?

Turning wacky ideas into great ideas sometimes takes an outside perspective. This happens all the time for us; one of us will come up with an idea, and the other will put their own perspective into it to make it work. Sometimes all it takes is another person's viewpoint. More on this later. You can gain another perspective by having life experiences also, that's why we always to try new things and immerse ourselves in other cultures. By looking at problems with your ideas from another angle, you will usually find the breakthrough you need.

Other times you just need to work through the idea to make it work. We often discuss ideas in the car on the way to work or sit down and brainstorm out the idea to come to a conclusion of whether it is worth taking forward or dropping.

2. Swipe Files

Slow hunches can often come about when you're inspired by other's work. Which leads us to Swipe Files. A swipe file is where you capture or 'swipe' something that has inspired you and put it away in a folder for later use. So it could be a particularly striking graphic that took your attention, or a well-written piece of copy, something that made you buy something, or some Stand Out Marketing Idea that blew you away. Either way, capture it, because when you are trying to think of some creative ideas down the line, this swipe file is going to help you out massively.

Again, use what you feel most comfortable with to capture and organise: Evernote for example is especially good for this. Pinterest is another way to do it; it's possible to set up a private board for your own use, and add interesting things to it. You can then even share it with graphic designers at a later date so they can see what your interests are.

When we're stuck and need some inspiration for ideas, we look back at our swipe file and immediately it helps the creative juices flow.

The reason why it works is because they're ideas that have worked on us, thus they are proven.

One of the hardest parts of coming up with good ideas is actually knowing whether it is indeed a good idea, and if it will work.

A great way to combat that is to see what's worked for others and do the same yourself - except doing it in your own way.

There's a caveat here: Don't put in your file swipes from your own industry. That's simply copying. We can admire what other people in our industry have done, but we would never directly copy, or you are just 'following the leader' once again. Taking inspirations from other industries and applying it to your own business is the way to do it.

3. Scheduling Time to Get Creative

It's important to schedule time to work 'on' your business, not just 'in' your business. By spending time working on your business, you allow yourself to come up with ideas to help with the business and how to improve it and make it more effective, so that you don't need to work so hard. In fact, the more you work on your business, you'll find the less you have to work in the business. Sounds good right?!

It's also in this time when Stand Out ideas can be brainstormed and put into place. As with anything in this life, if you don't make time for it, it won't happen.

When people say, "I don't have time" what they actually mean is, "I don't value this" above another task. If taking time to get creative will help you to become remarkable, Stand Out and help get your business out there in a way you can't imagine with anything else, then yes, taking time to get creative and brainstorm new ideas should be valued and time should be made for it!

Make time in your busy schedule each week (if not each day) to work on your business, get creative, and brainstorm ideas to help make you Stand Out.

Make time and it will happen.

But which time?

You can only be creative if you're in a good mood, that's why organising time is so important.

Being creative and getting yourself out there should be fun, but organisation comes first.

One of the biggest and most commons reasons why you're not in a good mood is because your mind is clogged up with all the things you have to do and whether you're behind on work, and all these other ideas that you want to look into stay in your head.

If you actually schedule the time when you're most productive (for us, this is first thing in the morning, never in the afternoon) then make that the time to be creative. If it's in the morning, don't check your emails and your social media accounts and then start, because you'll have 100 thoughts and conversations in your head distracting you.

You might have a flare of inspiration, but if you're being good and trying to be efficient, don't take time out to dabble with the idea, stick with what you're doing and get it done, because that's what will make you productive.

We would recommend however, writing it down to come back to later.

If you can get it all down you'll feel much better, because you can take charge of what you're doing.

One thing that we have done in the past, and what multiple business experts have also suggested, is to schedule in a much longer-term break than just a few hours or days, but actually take a full week off. No distractions, no meetings, no calls, just you stepping back away from your business to see the bigger picture.

At the time we had got to a point where business was coming in regularly (because we were using the principles of this book) and we were just doing work when it came in. But it wasn't what we always wanted to do, and if we carried on that way then we wouldn't have reached our ambitions and dreams.

In short...We had become comfortable, and that's the archenemy of ambition. We needed to get out of this comfort rut.

Take a photo of this and Tweet using #hippocampusbook

"ARE YOU STUCK IN A COMFORT RUT?"

thehippocampusbook.com
by @andrewandpete

So we took a week out.

Let us tell you it was phenomenal. It allowed us to see where we were heading, compared to where we wanted to be. It allowed us to focus in on what was making us money and what was wasting our time. It allowed us to make plans to get to where we wanted to be and achieve rather than just hoping things would happen.

After this time, we realised we needed to step up our game and work hard to achieve what we wanted. At the end of the week we had come out with an idea to really Stand Out in our market, we worked on becoming 'better' and had some 'remarkable' ways of Standing Out.

So we would highly recommend it. You will feel reinvigorated and at the end you and your business will be in a much better place. You can't just force creativity or Stand Out Marketing ideas, you need to time to breathe, reflect and mull over. Giving yourself time will help that process.

Some experts just say, go home now and book a week's holiday somewhere abroad. Now for us, that's not realistic or practical! Looking at our schedule we had to book out a week for this six weeks in advance. This allowed us to finish off and work around any paid work, projects, deadlines and meetings. It was tough and scary to do this because there's no guaranteed results at the end, but trust us - this is so worth doing at least once a year, if not every six months.

4.1. Brainstorming: Mastermind Groups

For many small businesses and entrepreneurs it can be hard to brainstorm and get creative all by yourself. So *don't* do it all by yourself, get involved in a mastermind group. Either join an existing one or set one up. There are paid ones and free ones but essentially the concept is the same. If you want to create a mastermind group, just download the Graduation Pack (www.thehippocampusbook.com) for everything you need including: email invite drafts, how to structure a Mastermind Group, and how to set appropriate guidelines to ensure everyone benefits from it.

The concept of Mastermind Groups was originally introduced by the author of "Think and Grow Rich," Napoleon Hill, a man who interviewed all the richest and most successful people in the world. He states that a Mastermind Group is: "The coordination of knowledge and effort of two or more people, who work toward a definite purpose, in the spirit of harmony."

How they usually work is that around four, mutually benefitting people meet up once every two weeks or monthly; each person gets an equal amount of time (e.g. 30mins each) to discuss their business and any ideas, problems or opportunities they have. Others in the group chip in, help and offer their perspective, before moving onto the next person. Each person also has to set goals to achieve before the next meet up and everyone holds each other to account.

They are great because you can bring up some of those slow hunches and brainstorm them together. This is invaluable if you work alone or in a small team. We would highly recommend setting one up with some business friends that you know. Tell them about this book and that you think it would be a great idea to sit down regularly as a group to brainstorm and hold each other accountable to our goals. You can use the group to get feedback on your ideas and you can help each to keep accountable. Make sure they grab a copy of this book too so you can all understand what you are trying to achieve! ;)

4.2. Brainstorming: Mentor

In the same vein as a mastermind group, a [good] mentor will help you in a similar way.

A mentor will ask you questions and share stories from their own experience, to help you find the answers within yourself.

In this sense then a mentor is highly recommended - especially if you are a one-man band or a small team. They can bring a different perspective and help you to think in a new way.

What's more is that when you have 'remarkable' ideas you can run them past your mentor to see if they think it is a good idea or not. You should probably tell them to get a copy of this book too so they know what you're on about ;)

You can pay for a mentor or you may be lucky enough to find a businessman or businesswoman to help you out of kindness and generosity. In general, most people want to help others if they can, and especially successful people - they want to give something back.

You cannot just presume this however, most successful people are too busy to just give away their time to a stranger. In that vein then it is most definitely worth asking someone you know or reaching out to someone in a nice way to build the relationship first.

Also consider, rather than asking someone if they will mentor you for free, why not ask instead if just once a month you could buy them a coffee and 'pick their brains' (awful phrase but we're going with it) for twenty minutes? It sounds much nicer and makes it a much more acceptable proposition than "Can you spend over an hour a week to come and mentor me please?"

Despite asking for only twenty minutes they'll probably give you longer.

When choosing a mentor pick someone who you think you will get on with, someone who you admire, and someone who has done what you want to achieve (or at least is on the way there).

4.3. Brainstorming: No Wrong Answer Game

A tip for brainstorming is to use the 'No Wrong Answer' game, that we often play in the office. It's based on the idea that quantity leads to quality and that often a wacky, off the cuff idea might actually form the basis of a great idea.

Typically when brainstorming you start by coming up with lots of ideas - everyone shouting out stuff to the person writing it all down. It is crucial at this point to keep everyone's spirits up and the creative juices flowing. If at any point somebody suggests something and then is immediately shot down or sniggered at, they won't want to shout out another idea again as they feel a certain amount of negativity. Negativity stifles creativity. The more bonkers ideas the better sometimes.

Essentially how the game works is that at this initial idea generation stage there are no wrong answers. Anyone who says 'no' or anything negative gets a yellow card (you can have actual yellow cards or just tot them up on a piece of paper), and the person with the lowest number of yellow cards wins!

Of course this isn't just an excuse to shout out lots of silly ideas. It is however a more fun way of brainstorming and cutting out the negative ninnies!

4.4. Brainstorming: Fill in the Holes

After the initial ideas generation stage you will want to drill down further.

Go through each of the ideas and pick out the ones that excite you most and expand on them.

This is where we play the 'Fill in the Holes' game. Some ideas will be awesome. Some ideas will have hidden potential but just need to be tweaked, and others need to be dismissed. But again, let's not have any of the negative stigma attached to having your idea dismissed.

Go through each idea and ask the person whose idea it was to say whether it's still relevant to the aim of the brainstorm. If 'no' then strike through and move on.

There will come a point where the silly ideas have gone and the good ideas and questionable ideas are still there. At this point we get to put on the black hat - that is to express concerns. This is a chance for whoever had the idea to defend it. Everyone can ask questions about it and the person can answer them until it is decided whether or not the idea is worthy of even further consideration.

Anyone can chip in to fill in the holes too. It doesn't just have to be the person whose idea it was. You should be thinking on the lines of 'OK, if we had to implement this idea, how do we make it work?'

This way, each idea has a fair chance and each idea gets to be checked for holes/flaws in them. If you can answer all the concerns about an idea then go for it! Even if the answers are more like, "I'm not sure how that will work right now but I'm sure we can figure it out."

With some ideas, they may seem too ambitious or too risky, but so long as you think the reward is greater than the risk, and it's aligned with your brand, then sure enough you can make it work with some extra hustle.

ASSIGNMENT

We want you to get everything in place so that you have the time to think creatively, so you can capture ideas for slow hunches and you have created an environment whereby you can brainstorm with others in a way that is positive.

Here's what you need in place:

Task 1: Have a place to write ideas down. Somewhere accessible to you wherever you are. This maybe a notepad that you carry around or an app on your smartphone. Personally we like the 'Reminders' App on iOS. It syncs to all your devices and you can have categories, further notes and place importance on each idea.

Task 2: Set up a Swipe File for capturing ideas that inspire you. This often involves taking photos, screenshots and capturing URLs of websites or articles. At the very least have a file on your computer dedicated to this. You can sync that with your smartphone using something like Dropbox. You may find that something else like Evernote or a private 'Pinboard' on Pinterest might be better for you. Whatever you prefer, set it up and into the habit of saving things to it.

Task 3.1: We all need time to work 'on' our business rather than 'in' it, and we all need to have time to think of creative ideas to take our businesses forward. You would think that the more you took time out, the further behind in work you would be, but actually it works in contrast: if you can dedicate time out, you make smarter, well-thought-out decisions that get you to your goals faster, your processes are improved so you can do more in less time, and you can think of creative solutions to become remarkable. Schedule as much time as you possibly can to devote to your business now. We found this hard at first, struggling with an hour a day, then we managed to do most mornings, then one full day a week, and so on. The batching of time really helps by the way, i.e. one focused full/half day is better than an hour a day.

So what can you start with? Have a look at your diary now and find a suitable time each week to dedicate to this.

Really push yourself to create a half day or full day somewhere. A top tip is to schedule this in advance; your diary may be full for the next couple weeks depending on how far ahead of schedule you are, so maybe start in a month's time the 'proper' dedicated time slot. For instance, you could say, starting a month today, every Tuesday morning I'm going to spend time on (not in) the business. From now until then, squeeze in time where your diary permits.

It will take time to get used to this but eventually everything will work around it. Don't ever schedule something in over when you should be working on you, treat it like it is sacred time.

Put a reminder in your phone/calendar now to reassess this every 2 months and see if you can squeeze in more time.

Task 3.2: We also want you to take a week off. This was invaluable for us when we did this. Try now to schedule this in your diary as soon as possible and work up to it. If it takes you six weeks before you can do this then that's fine, but just get it done. Don't put this off.

In that week, look at each part of your business (from branding to sales funnels, from cash flow forecasts to pricing) to reassess where you are and what needs to change, and what can you do more/less of. What process can you put in place to make things quicker/cheaper/easier? What can you outsource? How are you going to make more money? Are you reaching you goals? If not set smarter goals and schedule in time to reach them. Think about the bigger picture, are you on the right path? And perhaps most importantly, what are you going to do to become remarkable?

Task 4: Find someone to brainstorm with, either a mastermind group or a mentor or both. Either way, set this up as soon as possible. You will find lots of useful information, tips, and email drafts that you can copy and paste, in your Graduation Pack: www.thehippocampusbook.com.

SOM 105:
Conclusion

Don't Be Afraid to Fail

We think back to those first networking meetings we attended, and wonder where our business would be if we had been afraid to fail, if we had thought, 'No, we best not do that, people might get the wrong impression.'

Here's a question for you to ask yourself when you are afraid of failing...

... what's the worst that could happen?[1]

The cost of failure is so low these days there really isn't anything holding you back when weighing up the potential rewards to the 'what ifs' of negative thinking.

---

[1] Did you think of the Dr Pepper advert when we said this? Another brilliant example of how things are sparked.

We're teaching you a method whereby you can maximise more of you, and Stand Out in a way that is positive and within your brand values. As long as that is obvious then you will be fine.

Let's face it, you're not going to go wildly stupid here (we hope not anyway). You are aiming to Stand Out in a positive way.

Inevitably, change and remarkability brings with it people who love what you do, and others who won't.

Don't worry about those who don't. As we have said before you can't please everybody and they will probably just leave you alone anyway. Besides, you have something better now - fans! Embrace those who love what you do, treat them well and you will have fans for life. Your 'fans' will talk about you, give you referrals, not to mention spending more with you and give you repeat purchases.

In any story it is always the disequilibrium that drives the narrative forward. The good versus the bad. It's the same when creating a talking point. The debate about who's right or wrong gets people talking about you when you bring about change.

It's that divide that often brings about discussion in the first place, so embrace this Stand Out way of life and the word will spread about you.

Somebody who knows what it takes to go all in, and not be afraid to fail is John Lee Dumas, of EOFire.com, who now is one of the leading authorities in podcasting.

John decided to do a daily podcast interviewing the world's most inspiring entrepreneurs. The problem… when he decided to do this, the notion of a daily podcast was totally unheard of.

How could he possibly keep up that consistency, and reach out to the world's best and busiest entrepreneurs? Especially when he didn't already have all those contacts already. His family said he couldn't do it, his mentor said it was impossible and so did everyone else.

But that didn't stop him, he found a way, wasn't afraid and went for it. Within just a couple of years EOFire was turning over seven figures and his podcast was voted number 1 in iTunes.

He broke the rules of the game and did what everyone else basically couldn't be bothered to do… he stepped up his game.

So if we know the potential benefits, why are we so afraid? We think there are 3 main reasons businesses are afraid of being remarkable.

Ridicule

"What if I come out with my idea and everyone laughs at me? What if the press get hold of this and sneer? Worse still, what if people sneer behind my back?"

The point is, despite the message, more awareness and more people talking about you is only a good thing so long as you are honestly trying to do something positive. This is because it makes more people aware of you, and it's up them if they decide to like you or not.

So then it is up to you whether you have the confidence to believe in yourself, your values and what you are trying to do differently. If you believe in yourself, then so can others.

Don't be afraid of dividing opinion, embrace it. Use it to get more word of mouth.

Repeating our point from earlier... all the top Best Selling Books on Amazon also have the highest proportion of bad reviews. Isn't that incredible?

Be remarkable and some people will like it, and others won't. Either way you will get more awareness from people discussing you.

But risk of failure is so low. If it doesn't work then nobody sees. The worst thing that can happen is that you try something else.

Cause Offence/Bad PR

Whilst it is true that more awareness equals more opportunity to receive more fans as well as haters, to actively try to cause offence for PR reasons is never a good strategy.

Not all PR is good PR.

We don't need to explain further here do we?! Play nice, and don't use this book as an excuse to be offensive, or we'll set a real hippo on you.

Waste of Resources (time, effort, cost)

To become a remarkable business, to change the way things are done, to be innovative, often means change.

Pfft, sounds like effort, who can be bothered right?!

It's true, most companies aren't willing to radically transform their organisations, especially bigger firms.

Where small business can be agile and quickly adapt to the market, larger companies cannot. It's harder to turn around a big ship than a dinghy. This is where smaller businesses are going to have the advantage.

Blockbuster was in an optimal market leading position in the movie rental business - but in just a few short years they went bust, because they didn't step back and realise what was going on. They didn't keep innovating, they got comfortable. The rise of online streaming services such as Netflix and LoveFilm (now Amazon Prime) took them out almost overnight. They were remarkable - all the power of Blockbuster, but more convenient, cheaper, quicker, and more choice. Why have to go to the effort of driving to a shop, when you can just click and watch straight away? Blockbuster didn't innovate, it died.

This can be seen many times over. For smaller businesses, this struggle is often a long and drawn out process. Hope keeps them going. After all, without the expenses of bigger firms, you can survive for years just scraping by.

But who wants to just scrape by?

This is our point, if you don't innovate you risk suffering years of 'scraping by' before finally quitting. That's painful.

So why not be a bit ballsy?! If it's going to be tough anyway, why not try being remarkable?

Use the agile nature of a small business to your advantage to change things up and do something different to everyone else.

And if you think the cost of transformational change is too expensive or too much effort, then just think of the alternative - dying a slow death. It's innovate or die in this world. If you just keep doing the things you are doing then eventually the market will move on and your competitors will take your market share. Slowly struggling to attract clients to a dying, stagnant business is only going one way… downhill.

Here's the thing too. Most businesses don't invest in being remarkable. This book isn't going to change the opinion of everybody. Nor do we want it to. We want it to change the opinion of YOU though, because it is much easier being remarkable, when the majority of business aren't.

This nicely leads us on to...

Risky is the New Safe

We remember reading in the news one day about Rover, one of the leading British car brands. In early 2005 it announced that it would be making 5,000 of its employees redundant, with many more to follow. The story said that what's more, a further 18,000 jobs could also be also be lost from the suppliers of the car manufacturer.

Ouch!

Even when you think you are safe working in a large organisation with a reputable name, you are not.

You are never safe.

The only safety you have is the safety you create yourself.

Innovate or die. In this world being safe is actually being risky.

It's a strange paradox but playing safe now only means to be become stagnant and boring - which is risky.

Actually having the courage to be risky is exciting, fresh, and draws attention and business.

Risky then, is the new safe. Are you taking risks or are you just doing what everyone else is doing?

There's a great video called 'Entrepreneurs can change the world' by Grasshopper, and the main message is: Remember when you were a kid, and anything was possible? It still is.

> Take a photo of this and Tweet using #hippocampusbook

> "Remember when you were a kid and you thought you could do anything?...
>
> *You still can.*"
>
> Credit: Entrepreneurs can change the world - Grasshopper
>
> thehippocampusbook.com
> by @andrewandpete

You need to get back into that mind-set, like you had when you first started out and you were ambitious. You thought "Yeah, let's do this, I'm going to make lots of money and rule the world" or "Have such a great lifestyle", but then the daily grind takes over and that goes out of the window and you realise it's not that easy to run a business.

So the question is this, are you leading or are you just being a sheep?

In 2005, Turkish shepherds watched in horror as hundreds of their sheep followed each other over the edge of a cliff to their deaths. At first, one sheep went over the cliff edge, only to be followed by the whole flock. According to the newspaper, by the time the 450 had died, the pile of sheep carcasses at the bottom of the cliff had apparently grown large enough to cushion the fall somewhat, resulting in the survival of the other 1550.

If all you do is follow what others are doing, then you are destined to fail. You need to try new things and experiment with your own inner remarkability.

Don't be a sheep.

Do however take inspiration from other industries and put your own spin on things.

Do have the balls to go out there, do something different and make an impact.

And finally remember, being different means you can make a difference.

Take a photo of this and Tweet using #hippocampusbook

"BEING DIFFERENT MEANS YOU CAN *MAKE A DIFFERENCE*."

thehippocampusbook.com
by @andrewandpete

GOOD LUCK

Congratulations, you have made it to the end of The Hippo Campus. If you have been actioning the assignments as you go, or you intend to go back and action them now, the important thing is to action them at some point!

For help with this, and to download your Graduation Certificate, remember to go to:
www.thehippocampusbook.com, where you'll find:

- Templates for all assignments
- More inspiration
- Video content
- More practical examples of how The Hippo Campus could be applied
- Extra up to date information for all Hippo Campus students
- A vibrant community full of likeminded people.

The Hippo Campus is intended to be used, used once more and used again.

Use the principles of this book to make sure your business doesn't get drowned out by all the clutter, but rises above it all, like a gladiator riding on the back of winged, fire breathing mountain wolf, on a mission, and determined in its quest to get noticed, get remembered and most importantly, get motherf*****g talked about.

[Hey, who doesn't love a dramatic ending]

Soppy stuff.

So this is our first book, and we are feeling all emotional now it is done. Authors usually thank all the people who helped them write the book, but to be honest, we want to thank not just them, but everybody who has helped us so far in our business. It's been crazy fun, and the amount of people we would like to thank would fill another book we are sure.

Firstly we would like to thank every single person who has ever bought anything from us, including you if you bought this book (if you've borrowed it, don't be a cheapskate, go buy one ;), it really means a lot to be trusted working on your business, and bringing our own creativity to the table. Thank you to Lesley Calland, you saw something in us when we were green, and helped us develop that, you inspired us, and believed in us when we decided to 'go for it', and we will be forever grateful. Thank you Tiana Wilson-Buys for always giving us the encouragement and organisation we need to do all we want to do. Thank you Gudrun Lauret, who has been invaluable in making this book a reality - if you want to write your own book - go talk to her! Thanks to Ryan Branscombe for illustrating the awesome cover - you are amazing. Thanks to Aimeecarr, Titch, and Goose -

we don't see you enough, but when we do, you give us the best memories of our lives.

A massive thanks to our supportive parents and families, who are always there for us.

Vicky, I couldn't do it without you! A.

Kirsty, for putting up with me and making my tea. P.

THANKS FOR READING

for more visit: **www.andrewandpete.com**

Printed in Great Britain
by Amazon